Musings from Michael

MUSINGS
from
MICHAEL

An Inside-Out Look at
Gospels and Life

Michael J. Kennedy

 DeForest Press

Elk River, Minnesota

Published by:
DeForest Press
P.O. Box 154
Elk River, MN 55330 USA
www.DeForestPress.com
Toll-Free: 877-441-9733
Richard DeForest Erickson, Publisher
Shane Groth, President

Cover design by Linda Walters, Optima Graphics, Appleton, WI

ISBN 1-930374-20-8

Library of Congress Cataloging-in-Publication Data

Kennedy, Michael J., 1941-
  Musings from Michael : an inside-out look at gospels and life / Michael J. Kennedy.
     p. cm.
  ISBN 1-930374-20-8
  1. Christian life--Catholic authors. I. Title.
  BX2350.3.K455 2005
  242'.3--dc22
                              2005027161

To all those whom I was blessed to serve,
for I received much more than I gave.

About the Author

Father Michael J. Kennedy was born on March 20, 1941, in Minneapolis, Minnesota. He grew up in a poor, neighborhood to a family sometimes on welfare. Although an athlete and good student, Michael had a propensity for hanging with the rough crowd.

Gender and racial equality were taught at home and political discussions and campaign involvement were common. Hubert H. Humphrey, Walter Mondale, and Eugene McCarthy were among those who visited his childhood home.

Michael attended Catholic grade school and DeLaSalle High School in Minneapolis, then St. John's University in Collegeville, Minnesota. He left during his senior year for the St. Paul Seminary. In 1967 he was ordained a priest and became the associate pastor at the Church of St. Olaf until 1971. During that time he volunteered at the Stillwater Prison to people without family, was a board member for the Urban Coalition of Minneapolis, and chaplain for both the Daughters of Isabella in Minneapolis, and the Hennepin County Court and Jail.

He was an associate pastor at the Church of St. Austin from 1971 to 1975, during which time he was also chaplain for the Knights of Columbus, North Minneapolis Council. From 1975 to 1979 he was Director of the Priests' Personnel Board of the Archdiocese of St. Paul and Minneapolis. In 1978 he became pastor of St. Mary of the Lake in White Bear Lake, Minnesota, where he served for twelve years. Michael became Dean of Deanery One and chair of the Presbyteral Council for the Archdiocese and a board member of St. Thomas Academy in Mendota while guiding St. Mary's through a renovation project.

On a six-month sabbatical, Michael studied storytelling at the National Storytelling Center in Tennessee and went to Berkeley, California, where he met with a performer and director of the Berkeley Repertory Theater.

In 1990, Michael was appointed to his next parish, the Church of St. Patrick of Cedar Creek in Oak Grove, Minnesota, where he served for fourteen years. During his pastorate, he also helped guide this parish through a building project. He retired June 15, 2004, after quintuple bypass surgery, a series of strokes and other medical issues.

Back row, left to right: Eileen and Bill
Front row, left to right: Michael and Mary

Contents

Foreword

Those who have known Father Michael Kennedy throughout his almost forty years of a very active priesthood have known him as a priest of and for the people. During his priesthood, he has been involved in two very major building projects. Father Michael has had a special commitment to youth, the imprisoned and to others who have not had someone to stand up for, as well as to speak for, them. His sensitivity to the defenseless is powerfully expressed in his musing about the little child in the elevator who had not stopped crying on the inside.

Some, who will read this collection of musings, will be those who started reading them when Father Michael was serving in a downtown parish in Minneapolis. These readers will have followed him as he visited the jails, hospitals and effectively shared the priesthood of Christ with those of means as well as the poor and disinherited. They have followed his ministry through parishes, building projects and during the time that he served his brother priests as their personnel director.

Others may have only become acquainted with his musings at some point between his days in the city and his current "country home." At the time of this reading, readers will be aware that, after decades of helping others deal with their shortcomings, tragedies and disabilities, he has had to deal with his own limitations. Cardiac bypass surgery and strokes briefly discouraged him and limited his writing. However, it was not long before he resumed writing his musings and commentaries on the Sunday Gospel. During his convalescence, he made a special plea for the prayers of children and prisoners. He believes that the Father lends a special ear to children and prisoners, for his Son was one. Those who have heard Father Michael preach have benefited from his wit, which is seasoned with his Irish heritage. Hoping that it does not sound unduly sacrilegious, his storytelling ability is such that, if you close your eyes, you might think that you are sitting in an Irish pub or living room. Of course, some of this ability was honed during the many Sunday afternoons that he and his brother gathered in the living room of his parent's home to play cribbage.

Thankfully, Father Michael has sorted through some of his most helpful musings and compiled them in this most heartwarming book. He is a man whose love for all shows itself in his ministry and in many other ways in his life. And this love is exhibited in these musings.

JACK QUESNELL
Friend of Father Michael

Preface

This book is the result of a lifetime of writing and reflecting on life and on how the Scriptures apply to our lives today. It has been said that while most people look straight ahead at life's challenges, I tend to tilt my head and look at life from "outside the box." The result can be a new insight, or it might just be tilted and strange. Whatever the result, these musings cover almost forty years of being placed in parish bulletins "outside the box."

The following musings appeared in various parish bulletins, and for about the last four or five years have gone out weekly by email and have also been posted on the website of the Southern Dominican Province. As has been true of my parents and siblings, no one is neutral about the author, his writings or his sense of humor. I first discovered this at about the age of five.

A special thanks to those who served on the committee that babysat this book: Jen Schulenberg, Donna Kraft, Deb Landwehr and Lynda Keenan. Thankee!

How to Use This Book

As you'll note from the Contents page, this book covers Year B of the Catholic liturgical calendar in appropriate order, beginning with the First Sunday of Advent. This allows you, if interested, to prepare for the upcoming Sunday by reading the corresponding musing, or by reflecting on the lesson after you've been to Mass and heard the homily. You can also use it with a weekly study group, if you like, for the same purposes. This will help you discover the church readings throughout the year in a logical order.

To make the journey more interesting, each of the Sunday/Holy Day musings is followed by a more topical musing or reflection that spans many years and many issues, both public and personal. These may or may not have anything to do with the musing for each Sunday, but is provided to nudge, challenge, and help you reflect on your faith as you live it out day by day in the real world.

I wasn't there but others
were and they told others
who told others,
who told still others, and down
down the centuries and
finally someone told me.
Today I tell you.
You may want to tell others…

The Now Eternal
(1st Sunday of Advent)

In Latin it was called
Adventus
The anticipation
The coming
Of the Bethlehem event
And of the End of time
And the hearers were warned
Be ready
And on guard

But we are veterans now
Of many advents
And comings and goings
So one more
New liturgical year
Is just one more
Unless
A key can be found
To unlock routine
And ritual so familiar
We anticipate
Not much any more

Maybe
A key is simple
Just living
In the present
Not our past
Nor our mysterious future
Just living in the
Now
For now is
And
Now is

When
He
Comes
To
Us

Brigid

Why did you arrive
With such beautiful eyes
And that smile
Stolen from the sun

Within minutes
I'm sure
No more than a few
You grabbed my soul
In your open arms
And hesitating trust

You were seven
Or almost
You said
With dark and almost clean hair
The history of hurts
Never quite left you
As you said hello
To another non-dad

With all of our chatter
Which both of us know
Didn't matter
It wasn't 'til you
Gave me your hand
And held on
That I knew

Someday I hope you too
Know and understand
That once we
Crossed that line
As you huddled against me
So the world would be

More safe
Once I know
I had to say good-bye
To you
And no farewell
Has ever cut
So deep

St. John the Blister
(2nd Sunday of Advent)

Even after all these years
And all the readings
Classes and seminars
Still after all that
John seems
A tad strange
Or at least
A bit different

We know
He was fond
Of Elijah
And at least in
Word pictures
He also drew
From perhaps
Personal mournful
Desert experiences

Still he comes across
Like a relative
Who stays too long
Or a friend
Seemingly always
Grieving something
While his many laments
Drive joy from
The neighborhood

But it turns out that
While he first shows up
As a sore on the
Human heart
His insistence

On repentance
Reveals that he knows
Forgiveness
Will always be given
And stunningly
The blister
Evolves into a
Beauty
Mark

He Stopped

In the elevator
The little brown-haired boy
Began to cry
And then to scream

His mother hit him hard
So very hard
For such a little boy
But he did stop
Screaming
On
The
Outside

Mirror, Mirror, on the Mall
(3rd Sunday of Advent)

As long as
We did not look
Too closely
It was fun to consider
The history and culture
Of the people
Who saw and touched
Jesus or John
For at least a little curiosity
Was satisfied

And as long as
We did not look
Too closely
One could tell that
Even though John
Was just a cousin
He was also one
Who spoke without wavering
To those who had made
Their religion safe
And at a privileged distance
From the poor and
The hungry ones

And as long as
We did not look
Too closely
We could see
How different we were
From both the poor
And their oppressors
Ah yes it truly was
A fascinating game

Until at home or maybe
At the mall one day
We did look
Too closely
And we were so smug
We looked into
A dangerous glass
And then we saw
That we were both
The privileged
And yet still poor
At our depths
For in this mirror
We did indeed
Meet the enemy
And yes
It is us

Afraid

Sometimes strong
Rarely weak
Yet
Almost always around
Fear surrounds
Surprises
And
Situates us

An alphabet of things
Cast fear at us
From crime and cancer
Through appearance
And attitude
Being afraid
Firmaments
The human condition

The writings make a point
A deadly point
Proclaiming fear
To be in the heart
At its deepest part
The same writings
That library of books
Introduces
A simple
Child-like solution

For one
Only one
Will crack
The deepest
Darkest heart
Only trust

Or love
Or call it what you will
Meets fear
At its deepest part
Till always
Always
Fear Crawls
Crippled
Away

Waiting for Magic
(4th Sunday of Advent)

Important issues
Or seasons
Are often filled
With truisms
And tired expressions
Sometimes even in song
Which can be used
As protection
Guarding fearful hearts
While keeping dangerous
Admissions
About mortality
A safe distance away

So we prattle on
About best things
Being free
Or the
It
That life
Is supposedly
All about
And we wait
For revelation
By magic

And while clothed
In such superstitions
Or pining
For enchantment
Instead of life
We are reminded that
The maiden of Nazareth
Firmly and with

No trickery
Simply said
Yes

And became
The first
Who could say
Of her Son
This is my body and
This is my blood
And she didn't
Wave a wand
Or even
Play
Guitar

Pushing a Book

If things were a little different two thousand years ago, can you imagine the trouble the early Christians would have had in trying to get their message across? For example, if Matthew had tried to sell his account of the Gospel to a publisher . . .

Brring . . . . .Brrrinnnnnnng . . . . Brrrrrinnnnnnng. . .

"Hello, Caiphas Publishing House, Jack speakin'."
"My name is Matt. Is Patrick O'Hoolihan there?"
"No, Pat's at some religious gathering. Some retreat or something."
"Oh, I wanted to talk to him about my book."
"I'll have to do fella. What's the name of your book?"
"I'm not sure. I guess I'll call it Good News *or* The Way.*"*
"Not a very snappy title, Sweetheart. Can't you work something racy in the title somewhere?"
"Well, it doesn't really need a title."
"Doesn't need a title? Hey buddy, did you ever write before?"
"Well, no."
"What kind of work do you do?"
"I used to collect taxes."
"Take my advice, Max, stick to internal revenue, something you know!"
"But it's a fascinating story. Won't you just listen?"
"OK, OK, Mac, tell Jack about your masterpiece."
"My name is Matt.
"So all right. Tell me, tell me."
"It's about a man in Palestine who…"
"You want the Middle East section, fella, I'll connect ya…"
"But his influence is global!"
"All right, Mert, what did your hero do?"
"He went around teaching and doing good things for people."
"He traveled? You want the travelogue department, I'll connect ya, Max."
"My name is Matt."

"OK, OK! But you still gotta tell me what he said."

"He said you should love everybody, you should be a peace-maker, and you should be just and gentle."

"At the same time? Sorry buddy, that's not practical. That peace part would have been good last year. This year we're pushing ecology."

"But you don't understand. He's talking about a way of living."

"Living, smiving! That's a jungle out in the world, Mert. Your man's impractical, he's a dreamer."

"But he turned my life around."

"So I'm happy for ya. Hasn't he got anything else to offer? How about secret documents? Or did he ever cut a record?"

"I'm afraid I don't understand. You seem to be missing what I'm trying to tell you."

"Books, baby, books! I'm talking about what will sell. Don't you even have an expose'?"

"Well, I…"

"Sorry Max, but keep hangin' in there."

"If you could only…"

"And Mert…"

"Yes?"

"If you ever write anything on ecology or one of those 'tell it all' books, you just let old Jack know."

"But I…"

"See ya, fella, bye."

"Thank you, but…"

click…click…bzzzzzzzzzzzzzzzzzzzzzzzzzzzzzzzzzzzz…

The Last Shepherd
(Christmas)

When he returned
And they told him
About their vision
While he was in town
He simply did not
Believe them
Yet he went with them
To see the child
Not as an act of faith
But because he would
Do anything to
Get off the hill

Maybe that is why
When he saw
The gathering at
The place the child
Was resting
He was at first
Unable to speak
Not for reasons
Of religion
But just because
He was cold
From the wind

Later he wondered
Why he had been
So overwhelmed
On seeing all the other
Poor and scared people
Who came without
Force or threat
To visit the child

And finally
This last shepherd
Wondered why he
Was the first
To say what others
Of these forgotten folk
Were surely thinking
That the birth
Must indeed be special
Because he knew then
That the baby
Must be
God

The Deepest Hurt

To be feared
And
Or
Hated
Is hard to
Look at

But harder
Than fear
And
Or
Hate
Is to be
Taken for granted

For it means
You are not you
But a thing
Just a
Piece of the
Earth

Finding a Pouting Jesus
(Feast of the Holy Family)

We have heard
Or maybe even
Given some homilies
Reporting on the values
And ideals of the holy family
But strangely enough even
With every interpretation of
A Lucan method and intent
Still something else strikes
An important note that
Perhaps we should
Not entirely ignore

For when they
Casually begin and
Finally frantically search
For him they build up the
Possibility of danger and
Yet the story portrays a
Couple clearly constant
In their values of faith
And practice and also
Committed to a very
Nice reverence for
The one they seem
To have lost

Yet when
They find Him
With the big guys in
And around the temple
He turns out to have a
Moment or two of typical
Adolescent behavior and

Splendid planning about
Great and grand things
And even though Luke
Reminds us that He
Went home as a
Truly obedient
Son of Israel
One wonders
If they knew
They would
Actually be
Finding a
Pouting
Jesus

Downtown Ministry

A walk through St. Olaf's
any day
or
any hour
shows people showing some of themselves
to Him
but seldom to each other.

In pew 15, on the Second Avenue side—
a man, "getting warm";
no longer believing, no longer hoping
threadbare... "just getting warm."
A publican's distance behind
half-kneeling
half-sitting
mostly crying, partly choking,
a bead-ing widower,
if the rosary's out, why is he in?

Underneath the balcony, waiting for her bus
the legal secretary from down the street
shows him her ring
again.
Her fiancé's stag party will be
in Da Nang.
Their wedding may be in National or Gethsemane.

Over there near where JFK once sat
sits that "crazy woman."
She slashed her wrists last week.
Silently shouting
at Him
she wonders when
When
WHEN will somebody understand.

Lighting a candle in front
of the tabernacle
looking for all the world like
Marjorie Main and wearing white tennis shoes (I swear)
is the crusader.
Wonder who she's lighting a candle against today?
Maybe against that man
next to her
in front of Him.
He's black.

Down the middle aisle
a happy thing or two.
John is there.
His little girl is OK now, he must be
giving thanks.
Toward the main door
in the usher's row
a municipal judge
scales the day's decisions.
For openness and justice he prays
to Him
he knows will listen.

The vestibule
pamphlet rack, poor box, warning sign and all
stands empty now.
Soon
others will come in—
people—the same kind of
lonely, pained, happy
eucharistic people
now inside.
To many the church
and this building
mean much.
Others are "just getting warm."

How make it meaningful
to people
showing some of themselves
to Him
but seldom to each other?
How?
None of us even play guitar.

Mary, Mary, Not Contrary
(Solemnity of Mary)

Nursery rhymes are
Quite remarkable because they
Not only rhyme but also carry a
Meaning hidden in the verse
Much like the Twelve Days of
Christmas revealed a lot
As it passed along
Great truths of faith
And so does still
Another verse also
Born in England
Just a few
Centuries
Ago

It is of course
The famous one about
Mary, Mary quite contrary
Which goes on to allude to
Her garden which was simply a
Graveyard in which Bloody Mary
Had her Protestant victims buried
Thus giving the name Mary a quite
Mixed meaning for all time for it could
Mean an otherworldly monster but also
Could dehumanize the Mary of Scripture
Who is regularly victimized by her
Phony friends who almost deify
Her as if she only pretended
To be like other moms

So unfortunately
When we commemorate
Some of her feasts we may

Make too much of her
Thus making less and
Almost put her in some
Kind of "Quadrinity" when
We forget her trust and
Faith and that where
She has gone we
Might also reach
Since the truth is
We remember
Her for love
Making her
Mary, Mary
Forever not
Contrary

The Godchild

Dying is always hard
Even death
By symbol and sign
For dying like this
Invites life
To shine
And be shown
In living

To live after
The Font
In a new life
Means more
Than a shoulder
To lean on
That's Mom's or Dad's

It
This new life
That is
Means
A symbol arm
Or sigh heart
To call on
When Font's life
Needs help

It means more
Than Grampa or
Gramma or
Even a friend
It means a
Godfather
To say in
His heart and head

In this
My little one
You're related to me
For as a child of God
A godchild you are
For now
And forever

A Baby Named Herod
(Epiphany)

When the people of
Jerusalem are said
To be upset because
Herod was it can be
Quite comfortable
To sit in judgment
Over them or others
Down the centuries
Who have just gone
Along with those in
Power since when
We look back we
Can see the evil
And awful cost for
Millions of people
If the tyrant or chief
Claims divine right
Or allows no dissent

And when the crowd
Reacts whether out of
Fear or conviction just
As he would wish the
End results are almost
Always deadly at best
And since we know this
We scoff at the agony of
The king and the related
We-are-with-him anguish
Of all Jerusalem for we are
Very certain we would not
Have agreed to the killings
That inevitably followed

Yet before we accept
Too many medals and
Awards for our insight
We really should maybe
Honestly ask to whom
We are referring when
We grandly proclaim
Fidelity to the magi or
That we are gallantly
With the baby for
It may not be with
This Child born in
The town of David
But rather just a
Baby named
Herod

Joy

There is No
Joy
Like saying
Look at me
And
Then
Having you
Look into
My eyes
With
Your eyes

Thank You, Dad
(Baptism of the Lord)

It really is quite
Amazing how seldom
We praise our children
Or friends or even the
One closest to being
Our true heart mate
For it seems we are
Troubled by some
Dismaying anxiety
That if a nice word is
Even whispered the
Beneficiary will have
A head that explodes
From arrogance

But the gracious Lord
Who made us will have
None of this stupid worry
For He gives praise every
Single time He calls each
And every one of us one
Of His beloved children
And He does this every
Second of our lives
So it is like a never
Ending encore of
His pledging love
Again and again
And yet again

So perhaps
Instead of rejecting
The pledge of love
We need to seize a

Cue from this mentor
Who as he completed
Baptism by John was
Said to have heard the
Father say that he was
His beloved child and
Is it not likely that in
His heart the newly
Baptized one
Said simply
Thank you
Dad

Poor Man

He was hard to look at
that man who came to my door
last night
late
From his grubby hat
to his double-breaster
he telegraphed seedy Bogart
He was poor
and drunk
and dirty

Like over-done eggs and
late night parties
his aroma attacked the parlor
and took it over
when the air fled
As he introduced his hand to my shoulder
he stumbled on cheap wine
and sang-song to me

"A little cash to tide me over Father?
I must get home and see my mother"

"Money won't help you"
(I confidently claimed)
"You can't stay
On your way
and shape yourself up
I can't do it for you
I'm out of money
right now"

"You're out for yourself you priest
you never help the poor only the rich
Churches make me sick

and so do you
you priest"

But what about all our
commissions and committees
and United Fund appeals?
What about that poor man?

Shifting from one sweaty foot to the other
and promising to pray for him
I edged him
minute
by eternal
minute
toward the door and
explained how we couldn't give to everybody
that came our way
reasonable people don't expect it
certainly
he understood that

Suddenly surprisingly sober
and incredibly erect
he spit
in my face
and left

Hey poor man
let me explain
Come back
Let me
Hey poor man
we just can't
we can't
we can't
we can't
Hey
Hey poor man

Desert Dessert
(1st Sunday of Lent)

Not quite voluntarily
Since the account says
He was driven by the Spirit
And only recently baptized
In the Jordan by a cousin
Called John the Baptizer
The Master did spend
Some time alone no
Doubt pondering
His awareness of
The tough task
Yet to come

And from what
We know about Him
From story after story
And sign after sign his
Period in the desert was
Probably very unlike our
Own rueful Lenten time
Given that we so often
Gaze inside or outside
And wonder what we
Do need to change or
Have changed in us
Or maybe in one
Close to us

Instead He quite
Likely turned his sight
To the Father and asked
How He could take on the
Mind and heart of the One
Who sent Him and perhaps

This time around if we could
Only do even a little of that
And look away from self
And gaze near the God
Who really loves us
Then maybe this time
Our Lenten desert
Will lead to deeper
Discipleship and
That would be a
Special kind
Of desert
Dessert

An Exchange of Letters

Dear Father Realgood,

Just a note to call your attention to Ms. Flanagan's thinly disguised anti-Catholic article in the newspaper this past week. Those pro-abortion people keep insisting that only Catholics are against abortion. Did you see it? What can we do?
Sincerely,
Ima Christian

Dear Ima,

Thanks for your note. I did see the article and must say I was not surprised. There's a growing anti-Catholicism in the country. Somehow it's respectable to be anti-Catholic and to insist that there's a "Catholic conspiracy." What to do? Insist that public officials and the media be as vigilant about anti-Catholicism as they are against any other kind of group hatred.
Sincerely,
Father Realgood

Dear Father,

Is that enough? Can't we do something? Where's the Inquisition when we need it?
Sorrowfully,
Ima

Dear Ima,

Using force against hatred is as bad as using force against unborn children. We could use a boycott or, as a minimum, write letters of protest. It's terribly important that we be as consistent as humanly possible. We must be opposed to official killing as we are to abortion.
Hopefully,
Father Realgood

Dear Father,
I'm beginning to see what you meant when you said that the New Testament was more valuable and practical than the Tribune or the Star.
Love,
Ima

Dear Ima,
Amen! Hang in there, Ima!
Love,
Father Realgood

Molehill Out of a Mountain
(2nd Sunday of Lent)

Though Mark
Assures us that Peter
And the thunder brothers
Really did keep their mouths
Shut about what happened
On the mountain that day
When they saw light never
Seen before and got a hint
Of glory even they never
Dared to fantasize about
Still one wonders if they
Were silent because he
Told them to tell no one
Or simply because they
Missed the meaning
As they believed
Too small

So when they
Finally began to put
All the pieces together
And at last saw that his
Awful death was a new
Doorway to the life they
Remembered had been
Hinted at when he had
Spoken about his death
Then probably that trip
When the three closest
To him went up the hill
Finally began to
Make sense

For that time perhaps
They thought the light
Had been imagined or
At best a quirk of the
Sun on the shadows
Always present on
The top of that hill
Yet before they died
They must have been
Aware that they had
Missed what they had
Seen just as we miss his
Presence now so what
They really did was turn
The world upside down
As they became the first
Disciples to make a
Molehill out of a
Mountain

Coffee

A few weeks ago a man stopped the courthouse chaplain in the corridor on the fourth floor and asked if he would join him for a cup of coffee. Never one to turn down anything free, the chaplain accepted immediately. It was puzzling, though, since he was only on a "Hello, how are you?" basis with the lawyer who was inviting him to coffee. As it turned out, the lawyer just wanted to talk.

The five-minute coffee break stretched into forty-five minutes as the lawyer began to unburden himself. It seems he had told his wife about a case he was working on and in the process dealt rather loosely with certain things told him in confidence by his client. He didn't actually reveal any lawyer-client confidences, but he was not as tight-lipped as he should have been. He assumed, he told the chaplain, that his wife knew enough to refrain from mentioning anything about it to her friends. But that is exactly what did not happen.

Never known as a quiet woman (and in fact known for her foul mouth) his wife told a number of people about her conversation with her husband. She said later that she guessed she wanted to feel "big-time." Inevitably, her revelations got back to her husband's client.

As the lawyer was talking and expressing sincere remorse at having violated at least the spirit of confidentiality, the chaplain couldn't help wondering about this lawyer's wife. Every business, every profession and every church has a few members like her. They must be a part of all the "inside" information. They take great delight in telling "ordinary" members of the organization that they know more than the average person. When they are challenged, confronted or simply told to shut up, they are, of course, greatly offended.

The chaplain kept thinking (as he was having his fourth free cup of coffee) that keeping confidences is a very important virtue. Confidentiality is a hard won trust. It is so easy to lose that trust. And if we gain the whole neighborhood and suffer the loss of that trust, what profit is that? It made him wonder, as he finally volunteered to get the fifth cup of coffee for his new lawyer friend.

Sedation Ministries
(3rd Sunday of Lent)

Maybe this year
As we are half way
Through Lent with the
Easter vigil still before us
And as we get to hear the
Story again maybe this year
It will bring light into some
Part of the bleak darkness
That is present in the
Life of everyone
This side of
Heaven

Obviously you never
Really know what might
Happen at any given time
At a well for the woman
Who came that day was
Knocked off her feet as
Her soul lay bare in the
Hands of the magnetic
Stranger and from that
Moment she was on
Fire and full of a
Life beyond her
Best reflection
Or even
Hope

So maybe this year as
We once again see her
Bring a whole town to Him
Maybe this year we will look
More into our own souls and

Ask if like she and the others
We too could be eagerly alive
So maybe this year we will not
Take this news and once again
Package it with boring talks
And mandatory programs
Promoting more order so
That we end up not only
With a gospel that just
Does not seem to be
The good news and
Anyway is buried
In some kind of
Sedation
Ministry

The Man in the Elevator

Nobody ever talks
in an elevator
like many bottles
on a shelf
labels all straight
all facing front
The pain
of being by himself
all the time
becomes unbearable
beating him
outside in

The miserably metaphoric
waterless fish
and the wagon
without wheels
have community
next to him

Sometimes he feels
like a guide
on Enola Gay
leading to nothing
and nothingness

The sandy parts
of his heart
burn
The fire inside
is red
going on white

But the lower face
an unpaid gesture

an invitation
to greet
and the sand
becomes earth

The light of this morning
overwhelms the flames
the movement has
worked
He is touched
by the dream
of friendship

He talks
He speaks
He makes words
in the elevator

The Awful in the Awesome
(4th Sunday of Lent)

Awesome
Might be our
Modern response to
Finally being able to see
Like the one blind from
The very day of birth and
In the story we hear again
This year this blind man
Feisty before his healing
Was certainly filled with
Awe while dancing in
His heart and in the
Streets of beautiful
Jerusalem

But the pious leaders
Doused his soul boogie
With the waters of ridicule
And shame since as always
They presumed the healing
Was about them instead
Of a gift to the man who
Never saw before for they
Only observed the man as
One who dared disturb
The proper order of
Things religious

And then his parents
Virtually disowned him
In their panic about the
Same unsmiling leaders
Who were more worried
About observance of the

Sabbath than celebrating
The wonder of the gift of
Sight given by that other
Man from tiny Nazareth
So that by the time the
Man ran into his healer
Again he realized that
Within the awesome
Some people only
Find the awful and
Of course just one
More reason to
Hate a God
Who dares
To smile

To Three Dead Friends

Our songs are different now
Weary verses are common
Since you've gone
Speeches
Worn by meeting
After meeting
Stretch winter into summer

We lived on the hope
You gave us
Freedom and compassion seemed
But a step away
When
The bullets of despair
Brought midnight
And its friends
To our land

Brothers in heart
You pulsed the country
With care
And we were different
Somehow

The months-long ache
Is new each day
We want to cry
We want to scream
We want to pray

Late at night
When we hear your names
Or see your pictures
And only the silence
Interrupts our stillness

We remember
Your vigor
Your dreams
Your faith

And never
Ever
Ever
Do we want
To hurt
Anyone
Again

Dallas
Memphis
Los Angeles
Are dry
Dirty names

We miss you
God
How we miss you
Will spring ever come
To our land?

Lazarus Questions
(5th Sunday of Lent)

Was it a surprise
For you too
Coming from darkness
Deep in mother earth
Into the bright light
And center stage
Of a once lonely hillside

Did you cry or laugh
When you saw your friends
And their wonder and awe
And terror
At what your friend
Had done
In this wonder-work

Were you different
This second time around
Or did you descend
Again into routine
And taking-for-granted
Did you pass by the flowers
Or was your universe
Disturbed
Forever

Counting My Blessings

Being a priest
Being able to enjoy pizza
People in the parish who care
A pastor who shares instead of shouts
Pizza
Recognizing that I cannot come remotely close to carrying a tune
Relatively good fall weather
Kids in the school
The opportunity of working with Alcoholics Anonymous
Clothes that are too big for a change
Pizza
Teenagers in the parish who are not afraid to speak up
Blue Cross
Nuns on the parish team who are genuinely interested in people
A Mass schedule in which most of the Masses are at a decent
    hour
Knowing that Jesus is a brother and not remote
Breaking 90 once in golf this past season
Two alarm clocks that both work
Pizza
Parents who taught me to give my word sparingly and to keep it
    unfailingly
Keeping my Irish temper under wraps—most of the time
Air conditioning
A pastor who can cook
The lack of hypocrisy of the men in jail
The faith and loyalty of the people here
Short meetings
Weight Watchers
People who let me know, pro and con, about my sermons
Pizza
St. Austin's
Parents of our kids who care enough to listen to their children
Widows and widowers who are the real contemplatives of our day
Pizza

Every Silver Lining Has a Cloud
(Palm Sunday of the Lord's Passion)

When
The Master
Took the ride on
That sturdy donkey
With many cheering
And proclaiming Him to
Be the one who had come
In the name of the Lord they
Must also have anticipated
That they would soon know
With certainty that He would
Quickly be named King and
Then live in a palace filled
With plenty of gold or
At least with silver

But after they waved
The branches of palm
It became a tale that
Took a surprise turn
For the expected
Crown turned out
To be made not of
Silver but rather
Of thorns which
Cut into the One
So recently
Cheered

So the story then
And forever became
A dirty reminder that
Glory often follows
Only after suffering

Not because it has
To be that way but
Because we seem
To make the very
Same mistakes
Over and over
Almost as if we
Need to ensure
That absolutely
Each and every
Silver lining
Would
Have
A cloud

A Conversation

Brrring . . . . brrring . . . . . brrring . . . .

"Hello, St. Dymphna's Church. May I help you?"
"Father Realgood, please."
"This is he."
"Father, this is Ima Christian."
"Ima! Good to hear from you. Where have you been?"
"I've been out west, on vacation—in Colorado."
"Was it a good trip?"
"It was OK. The mountains were pretty. But I called to thank you."
"You—you want to thank me, Ima? What for?"
"Well you know I get on you sometimes for what I consider hair-brained changes."
"Yes, I do seem to remember…"
"But St. Dymphna's is not nearly as bad as some of those places I went to church on vacation."
"What were they like, Ima?"
"Well one place didn't even have singing! I even missed your @#x%! guitar!"
"Really?"
"Really! Another place had a hymnal—a pretty good one, I'll admit—but no missals or missalettes!"
"Are you sitting down, Ima?"
"Ya, Kid, why?"
"Well, since you've been on vacation, there's been one teeny-weeny change at St. Dymphna's."
"Get it out! What did you do now?"
"Well, we, er, ah, got a new hymnal, with over 200 songs in it!"
"Terrific, what else?"
"Well, we decided that the mis…"
"What, what did you say?"
"We decided that the missalettes should be phased out. Ima? Are you there?"

"I, I, I…"
"What's that crinkly noise I hear?"
"Just the wrapper on the tums, just the wrapper…"

Not the First Fruits of Google
(Easter)

When the wounds
Had just begun to heal
The first of many receptions
Was probably attended by
All those welcoming the Son
Home and applauding him for
His loving others enough to
Finally achieve a lasting
Victory over death

Undoubtedly Moses
And Abraham were there
As were Ruth and Jeremiah
Along with Judith and Joseph
Since each and everyone knew
And witnessed the great acts of
Compassion and sacrifice which
Finally culminated on the cross
So they must have cheered as
He was raised by the Father
And led home by the Spirit

And while some disciples
May still try to claim some
Things are beyond divine
Control and so insist that
His suffering and dying
Were just a haphazard
Attempt to save a plan
Gone bad because of
Sin the joyful party
When he did come
Home does refute
Such smugness

So rather than being
Just lucky or random
The death and life of
This first born from the
Dead is perhaps instead
The result of love beyond
Our own imagination and
Not simply a product of
One of our frequently
Used search engines
Nor even a first fruit
Of our adored
Google
Dot
Com

Memory

The memory of those times
Is sometimes clear
Sometimes so very clear
As the time
Goes by
And growing old is more real
Than a remembered time

The love that
Was born
So long ago
It seems
Is nourished now
Only in memory

The oneness in heart
That few ever know
Is a memory
To be saved
In the stillness
Alone
For remembering
Must see light
Again some day
For the life and the dream
Of the memory

The Divine Mime
(2nd Sunday of Easter)

At least as
John tells the story
Remarkably few words
Were spoken between
The disciples and the
Risen Lord during
Either of His visits
To the room where
They were hiding
For they did not
Overwhelm the
Leader with
Questions
At all

And maybe
Just shortly after
We perhaps assume
We would have acted
So differently from the
Disciples when He was
Arrested then tried and
Found guilty we in turn
Smugly think we at least
Would have deluged Him
With questions when He
Finally did appear

But in still
Another godly
Surprise He does
Not explain Himself
Or even His death and
Stays rather mum about

His time in the tomb and
The quite silent rising as
He was called to emerge
So by not shedding any
Light at all He seems to
Loudly shout just look
Hard at what I finished
And since it was done
For you and words
Will not explain it
Just let me be
The divine
Mime

The Fifty-third Meeting

Minutes of the fifty-third meeting of the holy family program
subcommittee of St. Dymphna's Parish

Father Realgood: The meeting is called to order at 1:00 P.M.

Mrs. Braddodge: How did you think the first public session went last
night, Father?

Father Realgood: Fine, but it's too bad more of the parents weren't
there; thirty-three out of ninety families isn't exactly a world
record.

Mrs. Braddodge: Give it to 'em on Sunday, Father, roast 'em good.
You're too easy on them. Threaten to refuse Christian burial, that
always used to work!

Father Realgood: Don't you think the people of St. Dymphna's are
tired of being yelled at? There must be a better way of motivating
them to see their responsibility.

Sister Caville: Do you play guitar? Can't do anything now days if you
don't play guitar.

Father Realgood: Why was the turnout so light, does anyone know?
Sister Fran did such a nice job; how could people object to such
a program?

Mrs. Braddodge: 'Cause people ain't reasonable, honey. You'd think
that parents would realize that they are the primary religious edu-
cators of their children. But no, they want to abdicate the job and
make Father Realgood and the nuns make little theologians out
of their kids.

Sister Caville: I think that they think the nuns are trying to get out of
work, not that I'm opposed to getting out of work, but they really
think that.

Father Realgood: Well, what are we going to do about it? There's
sixty some kids involved; the parents are going to have to do the
job. We'll help them as much as we can, but we can't let them off
the hook, we'd fail in our responsibility.

Mrs. Braddodge: Give 'em a little Harry Truman, let them have it!
Maybe we could raffle off a copy of the autobiography of St. Dym-

phna at the next meeting, that might draw a crowd.

Sister Caville: I feel sorry for the ones that were not there because they think they are so orthodox when, in fact, they might well be in heresy.

Mrs. Braddodge: Heresy! Those people—I don't believe it!

Sister Caville: Sure, the heresy of substituting theology for the faith and of elite private interpretation of Scripture.

Mrs. Braddodge: Should we call the ones that weren't there? That might help.

Father Realgood: I suppose so, but they have all received a letter, and there was a notice in the parish bulletin, as well as a pulpit announcement.

Sister Caville: Maybe those that weren't there can't read.

Mrs. Braddodge: And they wonder why their kids think that they are phony, here's a chance to communicate with the kids about something other than brushing teeth and they don't seem to care.

Father Realgood: Well, let's keep trying, perhaps we can reach them before it's too late. Should we adjourn?

Mrs. Braddodge: I still think you ought to threaten them a little...

The Best Happy Meal
(3rd Sunday of Easter)

It is almost
Beyond belief that
We often feel clever
When trying either to
Explain events which
Are beyond our ability
To understand or are
Just the problems or
Sorrows that scamper
Through most lives
This side of heaven

So perhaps the
Apparent gloom of the
Emmaus disciples and
The dreariness of those
They told who soon also
Had a similar encounter
Really does make sense
But when He came to the
Upper room where they
Were staying they finally
Listened as they allowed
Him to spend some quality
Time with them and like the
Travelers they too finally
Recognized that this was
The One who had been
Put to death only a
Few days before

And in a way they
Maybe never expected
The insight arrived like it

Had for those on the road
For again He certainly
Broke bread when he
Was right at the table with
Them and the breaking
And sharing became a
Forceful symbol that
Reminds us forever
That we find Him
Right in front and
In back of us when
We continue this
Breaking bread
For then and now
Even without fries
It still is the best
Happy Meal

Participation

In the last ten years, perhaps the most frequently used word with regard to our Sunday Mass has been "participation." The II Vatican Council urged that participation on the part of priests and laity was not just a "nice thing" to do. It was a necessary element in our celebration of the Eucharist.

For those of us raised with missals and with ears still red from reprimands for not reading our missals during Mass, the concept of active participation through singing, responding and listening came as a surprise. Habits are hard to change and the habit of quietly reading during Mass was hard to change. After ten years, is there now more active participation than before?

Clearly there is. Despite the need for improvement, most are now comfortable and happy with listening to the Scriptures (and they mean more than ever before!), singing our praise to God, and actively sharing in the celebration of Mass. Many parishes have helped their participation by strong emphasis on improving their singing by having a full or part-time music director. Others have improved their appreciation of the Liturgy of the Word by listening to well-trained readers instead of half-listening and half-reading the Sunday readings. All in all, the liturgy means more to most of us now than it did ten years ago. As we continue to strive for greater participation, we would do well to remember that the benefits of the last few years far outweigh the minor inconveniences.

Again, it is not a question of option for us. Our faith directly is related to good liturgical celebration. And good liturgical celebration necessarily involves active participation. As the American Bishops said in 1972:

"Faith grows when it is well expressed in celebration.
Good celebrations foster and nourish faith.
Poor celebrations weaken and destroy faith."

Another Musings for Mahoney
(4th Sunday of Easter)

You have been
My companion for
Over six decades
And you know I am
Very fond of you so
Please do not pout
When I ask again
About the sheep
And shepherd
Gospel images

And also give
Me some credit for
Understanding that they
Are good reminders that
We are never alone and
The master watches out
For each and every one
But why could he not
Have found an image
That is less cowering
Unless he wanted
Us to be docile and
Seemingly blind
In our following

But Mahoney my
Dear guardian angel
You say that he means
Us to also be shepherds
And not just obedient
Sheep and stay stuck
In pastures we trap
Ourselves in with or

Without planning so
Really you mean the
Shepherd role is one
Each disciple is called
To enter even though
In our frailty we are still
Many times just various
Itty bitty lambs purring
A baa here and there
When we are asked to
Stand up and be the
Dependable leader
Like a shepherd
In the clothing
Of a sheep

Surprise

Many are the days
And nights too
You know
That are routine
After routine
Without freshness
Or joy

To be filled with
Peace or joy
Or whatever that is
Presumes wonder
Rising up again
And again
In surprise and
Delight in many ways

That's why my
Bright-eyed friend
Your surprise
I love you
Is more than nice
It is the very stuff
Of life

Of life
My friend
Of life
So whatever you do
Don't ever stop
That grin and
Marvelous touch
When you sneak up
And simply say
However you do
I have a surprise
For you

The Itty Bitty Little Branch
(5th Sunday of Easter)

Sometimes
Words can be
Terminally cute or at
Least shallow enough
To allow us to sidestep
Reflecting on meaning
So we can pretend that
All is well when it is not
Since when we begin to
Believe that we are able
To be independent and
In no need of others we
Soon will discover that
The source of life and
Spirit seems to have
Been destroyed

It is bad enough
When this disjointing
Occurs in the world of
Merchants or scholars
But when it is a family
That is ripped apart by
Our own unwillingness
To accept that we are
Not the font of unity
It can bring sadness
And even death to
Hearts that are
Wounded

So when Jesus
Claims to be the
Vine and anoints us

As dependent branches
With each and every one
Tied to Him it means that
When we try to capture
Control from Him we are
As deluded as an ant on
Top of a floating log who
Thinks he is the driver
And we are about
As effective in our
Revolt against the
Tree by our itty
Bitty little
Branch

Thoughts While Watching the Rain

Yuk
Autumn has been beautiful.
Do leaves hurt when they change color?
How many people really believe?

Francis, Francis, thou shalt not throw at the opponent.
How many leaves in a bushel?
Who should I vote for?

Yuk
How many shopping days till Ground Hog Day?
Sacrament of Penance—who needs it? We do.

Should I grow a mustache?

Is it going to rain all day?

What would we do without Eucharist?
Why are forty to fifty percent of the brides and grooms uninterested
    in their wedding liturgy?

Yuk
Why does Mrs. Korte keep bugging me about returning that call from
    my dentist reminding me of my semi-annual check-up?

We should pray together more.

Rain, rain, pain, pain.
Yuk.

Love Is a Many Splintered Thing
(6th Sunday of Easter)

While love
Can be splendid and
Even energizing there
Still is really no money
Back guarantee that
What is called love is
Either the real thing
Or even a little close
To being anything
At all like what is
Revealed week
After week after
Week in the
Gospel

For manipulation
And its cousin control
Are often described as
A love pledged forever
In order to exert power
Over the one the tricky
Abuser still claims to
Respect above each
And everyone yet
The clues are clear
But often only later
When the hurt and
Massive harm are
Bandages worn
Not proudly by
The exhausted

For the love
Expected from any

Who choose to follow
The Master is never just
Turned inward or used
To divide and fragment
Others or even oneself
For loving as He asked
While coming in many
Disguises or clothing
Still is forever giving
And while always
Many splendored
This love is never
Ever a many
Splintered
Thing

Things I'd Like to See but Probably Never Will...

Jane Fonda with laryngitis
A Democrat praise the wisdom of a Republican
The war over with by this Sunday
Peanut butter pizza

A Republican praise the wisdom of a Democrat
An end to racism
Snoopy elected President
Peanut butter pizza

Twins, Vikings and North Stars all going all the way
An end to legalized extermination of the almost born
More candor from our leaders
Peanut butter pizza

Someone asking ME for golf tips
Less watering down of Matthew 5:38-42
Charlie Brown as Snoopy's vice president
Martha Mitchell with laryngitis
Somebody telling the superstars that they won't pay them any more
    raises
Peanut butter pizza

A movement to legalize celibacy
Archie Bunker with laryngitis
Dave Moore with longer hair
A day without an attack on the media
Bud Kraehling with hair—any kind of hair
More readers of poetry
Peanut butter pizza

Someone complimenting me on my singing
An end to the war today
Peanut butter pizza

Soul Cooties
(Pentecost)

On that first Pentecost
When the crowd heard
Peter in their own tongue
It was not only a gift for
The disciples from our
Amazing Master it also
Set the stage for many
Questions and quarrels
For generations
To come

For since then
Few have responded
So quickly and so well
To the gospel message
Preached to them so that
The basis for this seeming
Lack of response must be
Discovered so that the life
Promised can thrive today
And yet it appears either
Some human weakness or
Sin explains our response or
We are left with a solution
My sainted grandmother may
Have presented for she would
Argue with a conviction that
Only she seemed to possess
That somewhere in that first
Generation who heard the
Word in their own language
There also was implanted
What bad poets might call
Lice of the soul or what

She might call simply
Bad cooties

And just as those
Death cooties might be
Carried from a funeral to
Another home so soul lice
Or cooties lead us to put
Ourselves first and we end
Up with a spirit of our own
Doing and not usually holy
And so my sainted herself
Would say enough about
Sin already instead we
Should pay attention
To those mean
And sneaky
Soul cooties

Random Thoughts on Learning That the New Pastor Is a Bishop

Oh, my God!

Being Administrator sure didn't last long, and undoubtedly there have been better administrators, but did they have to send a bishop to straighten things out?

I wonder if he likes to take the early Mass?

Do they still wear rings?

I hear that he's fantastic.

What do you call a bishop now days?

I wonder if he likes pizza?

What does he think of associate pastors?

Do you suppose he likes to say the early Mass?

Just ten more days of power—*sic transit gloria mundi*!

Maybe I can talk him into going to Rome for an Episcopal visit—and taking me along.

The Northside should have had a bishop long ago.

I'll have to get my cassock dry-cleaned now.

Does he share responsibility?

Everyone says I'm the luckiest assistant in town.

Perhaps I could tell him that bishops always take the early Mass.

What do you call that big shepherd's staff that bishops have?

Does having a bishop as pastor mean that I do more or less?

Will I still be able to force my literary "gems" on the public, or do I stop publishing?

Maybe I could set his clock ahead so that the early Mass doesn't seem so early.

Oh, My God!

The Tone the Builder Rejected
(Feast of the Body and Blood of Christ)

How often does
God have to slap His
Divine head in frustration
When He sees us idolizing
Persons named and still
Sometimes unnamed as
They are again cheered
And encouraged even as
They seem to proclaim
That they know better
What people need
And what God
Really wants

And so with great
Irony it is again around
Early summer and when
This feast celebrating the
Eucharist happens that we
Hear one more time from our
Friends now returned home
Some awful tales about the
Guardians of the church
As they view it and they
Act like some sort of
Heavenly rottweilers
Protecting the flock
While issuing attack
Orders against any
Who are tolerant
But whom they
Consider liberal

But perhaps worst
Of all is that they
Presume to speak
For the Master yet
Give offensive and
Bleak invitations
When His favorite
Images around the
Table of plenty were
Hospitality and party
And yet they turn his
Earth so upside-down
By a mood so foreign
To him that they have
Managed to quite
Miraculously set
The very tone
The Builder
Rejected

Cookin'

Dough on the floor
Or ceiling
Or door
Means many things

Maybe cakes
Or cookies
Or possibly
Bread

But beneath
The trimmings
And evidence
There to behold
It means
The cook's helper
Is three years old

A New Foursome
(Solemnity of the Most Holy Trinity)

There might be
As many golf jokes
About God as there
Are arrogant ideas
And theologies but
Neither stories nor
Even good use of
The intellect really
Gets us any closer
To understanding
The divine mystery
Who is three and
Yet still one

It does help to
Humanize God to
Believe that on a
Golf course in his
Heaven God would
Erroneously think
He could hit as far
As Tiger or Jack or
Even Annika and yet
Our silly remodeling of
Him in our own image
Does not solve our
Problem of not really
Understanding this
Strange deity who
Is so full of love He
Cannot even fall
Into pride

But harder still
Than grasping
Any inner or outer
Workings of the one
And the three is figuring
Out the greater mystery
That this threesome truly
Does invite each disciple
Inside so that again and
Again forever and ever
With each disciple
This God always
Forms a new
Foursome

Ministry, O Ministry

After a full day of appointments, pre-marriage instructions, liturgy planning, committee meetings and more than one surprise, the Roman collar comes off and the radio or TV comes on. The exhilarating tiredness that comes from important work needs some time to ease away before sleep will be possible. On this particular night the parish priest grabs his phone messages and prepares to return the evening calls.

As he ponders which call to make first, he wonders how anyone could consider ministry boring or lacking in challenges.

The top message is from Mrs. M_____, the parish professional complainer. He's known her for three years and has never seen her smile or say anything positive. With a tinge of guilt, he puts off calling her 'til tomorrow. There's a message from John W_____. John's been in treatment for alcoholism and just got out. The priest reflects on the joy of being able to help someone turn a life around as he dials the phone.

John was never happier, and some of that happiness came through the phone. The next message is from a gentleman who is very angry because his son was refused marriage. As he grits his teeth for the argument he knows will occur, the priest wonders if this man really believes that the parish staff only works on Sundays. He seems to think that the refusal to marry was because of clerical laziness rather than the acute neurosis that the priest is sure is present in the son.

The call was much better than expected. The father agreed to come in and talk and is at least open to discussing help for his son.

With some guilt, the priest puts aside the messages for tomorrow. It's now pushing midnight and time for sleep. As he begins talking over his day with the Lord, he wonders again why everyone doesn't want a priest in the family. If they only knew…

The Original Rocky
(2nd Sunday, Ordinary time)

When people in our
Civilization hear that
Name Rocky spoken
Almost always a smile
Lighting up the whole
Body follows at once
As the image of a loser
Hitting the big time fills
The head and center
Of all who have been
Or have known their
Own piece of a rock

When the teasing
Invitation was given
To disciples of John
No one could have
Foreseen that Simon
Who after all missed
That first summons
Would be the one
Chosen to be the
Foundation stone

And this fresh rock
Given the new name
By the Word himself
Fits the mold as he is
Desperately ordinary
Reminding us forever
That we are not only
Called before we are
Worthy or maybe even
Aware of love and yet

We are invited into a
Life beyond dreams
For as worthless as
We might feel or as
Much as we would
Enjoy hiding in pity
We will be forced
To see that today
Since we are the
Riff raff alive now
Any of us is still
A more obvious
Choice than
The first and
Original
Rocky

Paragraphs

Not long ago
though
like years it seems
a little move
a small smile
were
mountain-like
in the awe
they gave

Yet
From squeals
and noises
words began
to come
then
more words
and
more words

Almost
overnight
it seems
that little
helpless bundle
was talking
in paragraphs!

The Good, the Bad, and the Snuggly
(3rd Sunday, Ordinary time)

Even after
All these years
It is still a delightful
Surprise that the Master
Chose ordinary and even
Snubbed people to be the
Bearers of the good news
Thus adding a little spice
To His message of
Love and justice
And peace

Once again we
Can stand in awe
At His courage in
Not recruiting either
The super religious
Or the very important
And wealthy ones who
Could have supported Him
Without a capital campaign
Instead He chose the ones
Often looked down upon
Like shepherds and some
Tax collectors and those
Ridiculed and scorned
Fishermen who at best
Were just ordinary and
At worst could make
A Herod seem ready
For canonization

The real miracle
Might not be either

The healings or mercy
Surrounding this one
From a small village
It just might be that
He turned them into
Fishers of men and
So the good the bad
And the ugly were
Changed forever
Into the good
The bad and
Yes the
Snuggly

Serendipity

After so many readings
and so many words
you'd think we'd begin to see
it's the unexpected
to expect.

He won't be trapped
or cornered
He'd rather surprise us
as friends often do.

Rome or Jerusalem
would have made sense
but who would guess
David's town?

He's still here
you know
in our midst
in the city
He's the one
you're sure
he isn't.

Make Cows Fly
(4th Sunday, Ordinary time)

Some things seem
So impossible they are
Easily dismissed but when
It turns out they are true we
Become speechless or reject
What is right in front of us
Interestingly it is the kind
Of denial that ran rampant
Through the tale about the
Emperor who had no
Clothes so that when
We refuse to accept
Jesus at his word
He must stare as
We stand with
Naked hearts

When He calls
Disciples to be poor in
Spirit and in many other ways
On His list of things to do or to
Be the reaction from the first
Members He called and even
Our response today is likely to
Be a polite assent but no belief
For like those called many years
Ago we are convinced that we
Live in the real world not in
Some fantasy one
However pious

And yes once again
We have forgotten our
Experience of the Lord in

A spouse or a child or a truly
Welcoming community or in the
Simple and uncluttered wisdom
Which fills an old friend or even
When we help others mourn
Then finally when we do
Remember our Jesus
Roots we know that
Somehow sometime
He could even
Make cows
Fly

Fifty Years

On October 19, 1933, a young man and woman promised their love forever as they were married in a little country church in Corcoran, Minnesota.

The economic times were awful as the Great Depression took hold. Within nine years they had four children, moved to the city and the husband was drafted into the Navy (at the age of thirty-four, with four children). They survived the battles of the war, the Depression and settled in to raise a family. Their four children all went to college and became professionally an attorney, an anthropologist, a real estate and marketing expert, and a priest.

The hidden sufferings known only to them, the openness to God's grace and their rock-hard faith in God and in each other developed them and their marriage into a beautiful witness for those who know them. Not only do their children love them, but they are tremendously proud of them. Them? That young couple? They are my mother and father, married fifty years ago this past week. Congratulations!

What We Get
(5th Sunday, Ordinary time)

We would have been
Brave and never have
Run away when things
Got treacherous if we
Had been able to hide
And carefully watch the
Lord work and teach and
Heal for a day or two for
We then would have
Known for sure that
He really was the
One sent by God
To save us

So maybe we
Get a little jealous
And judgmental as we
Listen as Mark walks us
Through a day of ministry
And we see that while some
Marveled at his power and
His speaking with authority
They also walked or ran
When things got difficult
And finally even deadly
And so we just know
If we had been able
To really see him
We would have
Stood fast

But of course
We dangerously
Fool ourselves and

Others since we do see
Him all the time in the least
Among us and in the daily
Caring and giving eventful
Revelations we encounter
So our holy laments about
If only this or that are
Hollow when really
We just need to be
Aware that what or
Who we see is
Who and what
We get

Father

When the hurt
begins to beat
and beat
when tears
need dabbing and drying
and strength
screams out its
invitation
he's one you
must turn to

When hardness
and coldness
surround you
from side to side
and front to back
gentleness beckons
and solid ground
you hasten

For it's the father
or dad
in the father's plan
who with his love
must take your hand
and guide
and lead
through no man's land

"To father"
is more than a verb
or function of biology
it is a challenge
and task
a charge to be

strong
in love and hope
and most of all
just maybe
it's a charge
to lead gently
gently
through the night

The Jesus Secret
(6th Sunday, Ordinary time)

If it really did happen
The way described by Mark
Then the thoughts must have
Zigged and zagged for any
Who saw or knew the leper
Had been cured and then
Been quickly told to keep
The news quiet and even
If it was just a literary
Device it still gets a
Lot of interest today
Since no one could
Seriously keep
This secret

But in this age
Of tabloid religion
And sleight of hand faith
It is somewhat consoling
That the author had to be
Concerned with a bit of
That too as people got
Fixated on the healings
Or miracles and missed
Even seeing the maker
Behind all wonder
Then and now

So too there are
Those among us today
Who long and pine for
A little magic instead of
Trust or for the dramatic
Instead of the routine

Of ordinary service but
Perhaps there is some
Comfort in seeing that
Others before also
Missed the point for
It never was healing
Or stardom or praise
But just giving love
Even to death that
Always was the
Real Jesus
Secret

Musing on Musings

What do you call
Those things you write
The voice on the phone
Asked somewhat
Aggressively
They are not prose
Nor poems like
I once learned
They're kind of
Raves and rants
And essay-like both
Poems and prose
So are they
Proems

Not to make
Too fine a point
Or to knock
A nose out of joint
I wistfully replied
Not to contribute to
The verbing of America
But of ancient lit
They are products
Of the wee little
Spirit within once
Called a Muse
Therefore
Musings

Before you object
Or are inclined
To complain
Hey it could have

Been worse since
That wee little one
Inside could have
Had a different name
Perhaps like
Ramble

The Buddy System
(7th Sunday, Ordinary time)

Maybe
Just maybe the
Best part of the story
About the guy lowered
Down through the roof
Is that it was apparently
The belief of his friends
That led to his cure and
Even to this day there is
Debate about whether
The man himself had
Even a little faith

Since it is unlikely
That any conviction of
The one who was healed
Was accidentally omitted
One has to wonder what
Exactly the author was
Trying to demonstrate
About the role of faith
In the healing ministry
Done so often by this
Nomadic teacher from
That tiny Nazareth

After all the Lord
Often tells someone
That his or her faith
Has really saved them
So perhaps here Mark
Simply exults in the fact
That the faith of others
Is also significant and

Since we are now all
Members of this family
Of God and thus really
Brothers and sisters
What we do and what
We pray for others
Matters beyond our
Own weakness so
Perhaps this was
And is the best
Buddy system
Ever and
Forever

Stars

Many are the mysteries
Of earth and sky
Many are the questions
Of now and then
Many are the answers
Near and far
But none so
Puzzling
Really puzzling
As one flickering
Star

When the air is clear
And no clouds intrude
They speckle the sky
And won't go away

We wish on them
Curse them
Hope and wonder
On them
But never
Never do we understand
Even one

To be on your back
On a very clear night
Is to know wonder
Awe
And even fright
For they are
Friends or foes
Depending on us
But whether that
Or this

They are
They are
They are
And so
Are
We

Wine Skins of the Kingdom
(8th Sunday, Ordinary time)

Party time
All the time was
The charge against
The Master and we still
Hear it again and again
In the weepy whine of
Those who thought the
First disciples were not
Austere enough when it
Came to fasting or the
Other ways one could
Flaunt pious virtue

But rather than
Giving in to them as
Usually happened when
Faced with the contempt
They consistently would
Disguise as wise concern
The Lord simply reminded
Them that change was not
Only here to stay but quite
Crucial and necessary so
They might stop trying
To fit the new law into
Their own set of rules
Or old structures

And while they must
Have been appalled at
His clearly unholy pitch
Since they were in their
Own minds at least way
More virtuous than God

Still one wonders if the
New struggle was really
Not fear of a new direction
So much as it was the panic
Of losing forever those old
Religious skins that they
Controlled since suddenly
The new law required
That the whine skins of
Righteousness give
Way to the new
And better wine
Skins of the
Kingdom

The Last Year

The first time
Was a surprise
Like—
Almost like
A sudden rush of wind

It began as a tiny
Tiny thought
That this will be
The last time
With what will be done
By me
Here
In the last year

A year's celebration
Rejoicing in almost
Twelve years
Of being
"In the midst"
Suggested the Spirit-man

Good idea
Wonderful
But
But
In the middle
During this
Celebrating year
Of what has been
And it has been
There will be
Times of hard letting go
Of
Cardiac ouch

But that's OK
OK
OK
It has been
That important

Shortcut to Nothing
(9th Sunday, Ordinary time)

Ever since humanity
Crawled from the cave
And began to explore
The world about
We started
To look for shortcuts
And so we cut corners
Here and there
And yet again

Until suddenly
It is as if we were driving
And took our eyes
Off the road
Just for a second
Only to turn back and see
A truck bearing down
And we found
Impending disaster

For it is clear after all
That the cloak
Of the Pharisees
Did not wear out
In the first century
But has been
Handed down
To each generation
For we still find comfort
In making rules
The shortcut of choice
Since we then can
Feel entitled to
Some kind of reward

And from the kingdom
Of His Father
The Master tries
To remind us
That rules
Bring order
But only He
Brings
Life

A Lament

A woman
And a man
And a child
Have disappeared in Chile
And Soweto
And Derry
And everywhere
The Junta masquerades

In the dark
The deep dark usually
When the wind
And their guard is down
They go
And go
Without request

And the Junta
And the Junta knows
And the Junta knows where they are
Living and hiding and dying
In Chile
And Soweto
And Derry
And everywhere

Their names are legion
Like the scriptural kind
Too many to remember
Or bring to mind
And
The Junta knows
The Junta knows where they are
The Junta knows where they are
Living and hiding and dying

In Chile
And Soweto
And Derry
And everywhere

A woman
And a man
And a child
Have disappeared
And isn't that
At least as important
As a building
Or program
The Junta
The Junta knows

The Devil Could Not
(10th Sunday, Ordinary time)

Many times when
We are caught doing
Something wrong or even
Just stupid we search for
Someone to blame and as
A last resort we invoke the
Devil or Satan to charge
As the one behind
The offense for
It would be hard
To prove he was
Not the culprit

The religious leaders tried
Very hard to get the Master
To act on their bidding and
Finally tried to blame Him
By calling Him an agent of
Satan himself until the
Lord pointed out the
Flawed logic fixed
In their brains
And once again
He did not
Make them
Happy

But the pattern
Becomes clear that Jesus
Is so focused on His mission
And announcing to the great
Unwashed that they are family
To Him so much so that He lets

His mother wait and so if even
She could not distract Him
Certainly then the devil
Could not

Betting Is a Risk

In any history of winners and losers, it will not be recorded a big loss. It may not even be considered a small loss, but a loss it was.

The fifth grade basketball team, having won two games by the scores of 8-5 and 16-14 and having lost two games by the scores of 47-2 and 31-4 prepared to play its fifth game.

Seeking to motivate them, one of the coaches said that if they got twenty-two points (an impossible dream thought the wise old coach!) he would grow a beard.

Clearly it was more possible for cows to fly or dogs to talk or, or, or the United States to beat the Russian hockey team… You guessed it—the pastor did not forget to shave today, he has to pay off a bet to twelve fifth graders. Oh yes, we lost the game 33-22, but did they ever play well until they got that twenty-second point. So if you don't recognize one of the celebrants for a few weeks, it is not Gabby Hayes.

The moral of the story? Never lead with your chin…

The Extraordinary Broadcaster
(11th Sunday, Ordinary time)

Even if one did
Not grow food for
A living it does not take
Hands-on experience to
Know that seed wasted
Is food missed so just
About everyone knew
That seeds were
Planted very and
Even extremely
Carefully

And when seeds
Were scattered it was
Done in a controlled way
But in this parable the Master
Makes the point that the seeds
Were thrown pretty much all
Over the place and the lesson
This story teaches might
Just be that like the
Farmer we too do
Not know why the
Seeds grow

By the end of
The story we notice that
The farmer seems to not
Worry about where the seeds
End up for he knows there will
Be a great harvest since behind
Every farmer is the Creator
Of all so the casting of seeds
Is generous beyond measure

Because the ultimate
Farmer is the first
Extraordinary
Broadcaster

He Ain't Heavy, He's My Brother

Author: I want to say something about my brother.

Reader: Nobody cares, big shot.

Author: But he's under attack in the media now.

Reader: Big deal—oh, all right, go ahead, it's your column.

Author: His term as chief public defender ends this year and the newspaper stories indicate he may not be reappointed in our neighboring county.

Reader: Has he done anything impeachable?

Author: No.

Reader: Why is he in jeopardy then?

Author: It is said that he is abrasive and doesn't realize he works for the county.

Reader: Is he—be honest now—is he a jerk?

Author: Well, let me put it this way. He is abrasive and very vocal for his clients, who are the poor and indigent.

Reader: You mean he's being charged with being too much of an advocate for the poor?

Author: You got it.

Reader: Nice charge.

Author: I thought so.

The Boat to Be In
(12th Sunday, Ordinary time)

It is kind of
Funny how people
Grow up in so many
Different ways and with
Attitudes which are carried
Into adulthood and sometimes
Even a surprise to the man
Or woman who discovers
Them only in trauma or
In great joy

One of the
Messages which seems
To be imprinted on the soul
Is the fear we all have when
Something is beyond our control
And so deep it can be that it
Nearly paralyzes us and
Almost always deadens
Our mind and courage
When they are most
Needed and
Desired

So the image of
The disciples being
Tossed about in a storm
They cannot control brings
Fear even to listeners but
We do need to not miss
The message that Jesus
Is always with us and
Where He hangs out
Is the boat
To be in

Croutons

There are times
When every phone call
Every dialogue
Even the hint of conversation
Deals danger
And fear and the furious
Promise of more
Really leading to down times
Depression
And solid scary vibrations
Even from those
Who say they care

The blues
As the lyricist
Proclaims this
Feeling of hopelessness
Fatigue
And once-in-a-while
Guest
Are always
Awful
And usually
Limited in duration

The solution
If that is the word
Though one wonders
Is the memory
Of non-blues
Happy times
And things
But mostly the
Memory of love
Esteem and

Even satisfaction
Simple satisfaction

The problem and the dilemma
Is the memory
Washes away
When the blues
Enter in
And nothing
Good or noble
Nudges into the midst
Of that irregular
Vicious visitor

The salvation
And that is the word
Is wrapped around
Friends and close ones
Who become memory
When the blues
Betray our own

But the surprise
For us
As for generations before
Is that
Our God
Surfaces
And surprises us
Since
The memory
Unveils Him again
And
His love
Comes through
The remembering
Done for
Us
With friends

Really Ridiculous Ridicule
(13th Sunday, Ordinary time)

It is not really
Too surprising that signs
And wonders are quickly
Dismissed by those who only
Pay lip service to the possibility
That miracles might actually
Happen and also denigrated
By the ones seeking magic
Like images in a toasted
Bun or in a field
Blown through
And through
By the wind

But when
Staring at a real
Miracle that others might
Try to explain away the
Disciple perceives also with
The eyes of the heart and
Faith which allow that some
Things really have no ready
Nor quick explanation for
There really is some
Stuff we truly do
Not understand

So really how do we
Imagine the crowd out front
Responded when the healed
Little girl walked out with
Her beaming family with
Her but is it too rude
To hope someone had

The guts to say to
The others that it
Was a really
Ridiculous
Ridicule

The Movement of Human-song

In the darkness
Of the moment
Or event
The blackness becomes
Reality

Historic hope
Fades gradually
And slowly gives way
Without much war
To sadness and desperation
or the growing grayness
Of emptiness

Yet
And yet
In the middle of the quiet fury
Is a memory
Vague and barely alive
Of life and death
And gain from loss
And a crazy sharing
Of humanity

For darkness itself
Is on ramparts of light
While desperation
Whispers memories of joy
And through a friend
Or the Word
The scream
Catches in the throat
And
Alleluia
Is announced again

Terminally Ordinary
(14th Sunday, Ordinary Time)

We may never
Find out how much
Was envy and what
Part might have been
People just so used to
Existing with regularly
Being belittled that any
Success by one from
Their very own place
Would seem quite
Unlikely and even
Impossibly
Stupid

So the folks
Who knew Jesus
From long ago and
Even up close as they
Grew together at least
In age and grace finally
Refused to be open to
Seeing what others saw
Or hearing what they did
And so rejected Him as
The prophet so closely
Followed by others
From different
Towns

But before we
Get all virtuous or
Smoothly pious we do
Need to remember that
We too would be much

More magical or majestic
If we had his role or power
For after all they dismissed
Him for the same reason we
Too reject Him in the common
Folk among us for like them
We know how much easier
It is to handle a divinity
Visiting from another
Planet than it is to
Deal with one who
Is just like us and
Who is also
Terminally
Normal

Changing Christmas

Brrring. . . . . Brrring. . . . . Brrrrrrrrrrrrrrrrring.

"Hello. St. Dymphna's Rectory."
"Let me talk to the young one."
"Pardon me?"
"The little one, Father Realgood."
"One moment, Please. I'll ring him in."
Bzzzz.
"This is Father Realgood."
"I hear by the grapevine that you've done it again!"
"Good afternoon, pardon me?"
"You've changed Dymphna's Christmas!"
"Who is this?"
"This is Ima, Reverend Goldentongue, Ima Christian."
"Well, Ima, long time no see; haven't heard from you for hours! What's on your mind?"
"I hear you're taking the wire out. 'Dymphna's wire.' The ONE I ALWAYS DONATE!"
"Well it doesn't really fit in with the Midnight Mass, Ima."
"Fit in, mit in! We've always used 'Dymphna's wire.' It's absolutely beautiful. Maybe you don't know the tradition behind it. You should…"
"I know the history of it, Ima, but I…"
"It all started when Father O'Hooligan was pastor, about thirty years ago. He wanted to add something in honor of St. Dymphna at Christmas."
"I've heard the history, Ima, and I don't…"
"So he got this beautiful idea of putting in…"
"Why don't you tell me about it, Ima…"
"…of putting in flashing lights and this wire which stretched the length of the church, from the balcony to the crib at the communion rail."
"There's not much use for it in the new liturgy, Ima."
"Then, at the height, the very height of the service, the lights would flash and get brighter and brighter and…"

"It sounds indescribable, Ima."

"And then from the balcony the statue of baby Jesus would sail down the wire—all the way to the crib."

"Oh."

"It was fantastic, Father. Right at the elevation, the lights getting brighter and brighter, then zzzzzzzzzzzzshshshzook!! Right in the manger."

"You're right, Ima, it sounds fantastic—but we're not going to do it. The new liturgy is much more simplified."

"You're taking all the BEAUTY out of it, you clerical simplifiers. That wire was always named in honor of St. Dymphna."

"We'll name something else for her, Ima."

"The person who donated the wire used to get thanked in the parish bulletin. Everybody is going to be disappointed."

"Well, Ima, we're going to have a simple concelebrated Mass and we'll sing lots of Christmas carols."

"But poor St. Dymphna, what about her Christmas, it won't be the same!"

"I hope not."

"What did you say?"

"I said it's getting hot for this time of the year, Ima."

"Well, are we or are we not going to send baby Jesus down the wire? Answer that!"

"Merry Christmas, Ima."

"It's beautiful…zzzzzzzzzzzshshshzook!"

"Ima?"

"Yes?"

"Merry Christmas."

"Merry Christmas, Kid."

The Gentle Dust
(15th Sunday, Ordinary time)

The order to
Shake the dust in
Visual protest against
Those not welcoming to
The clearly brave group
Of wonderful disciples
Might seem strange
When we first read
Or hear about it
And then try to
Figure out how
To really do it

And yet in the
Context of the many
Different ways religion
Has been jammed down
Throats instead of being
Fed into opening hearts
This is a pretty sensitive
Reaction to rejection for
It is as if the Master did
Know that if given even
A few opportunities the
The disciples would say
Any negative reaction
Should be enough
Reason to at least
Dispose of some
Of those quite
Ungrateful
Wretches

For even then
He sensed that
We needed to be
Always reminded that
It was not really about us
But rather it was about the
Good news being snubbed
And the way to change that
Would never be the sword
Or hitting them with noisy
Charges of ingratitude
For far better would
Be a soft continuing
Invitation by simply
Setting down some
Caring love in
The form of
Gentle
Dust

Things That Should Be Done This Summer (But Probably Never Will)

Finally do the spring cleaning
Read that book I've been putting off
Resist playing golf except on the day off
Celery *si*, pizza no!
Take more time for prayer
Volunteer for the early Mass
Be nicer to people who disagree with me
Visit the hospital more
Celery *si*, pizza no
Break 90 in golf
Get more feedback on sermons
Avoid scheduling summer meetings
Find out who that man is who drives here from South Minneapolis
　to hear my sermons
Avoid that man who says my sermons stink
Celery *si*, pizza no
Drive better
Read scripture more often
Celery *si*, pizza maybe

Wasting Time With...
(16th Sunday, Ordinary time)

The times we value
After they have come
And gone are often the
Very ones we resisted
When they were first
Offered especially the
Times we might have
Used to step back or
To take a break so
We could get and
Look at some
Perspective

But quite often
We feel pressure to
Take action and bring
Salvation or rescue to
Our world at this very
Point in time and by
God we swear that
This means now by
This or that plan or
Program and so we
Seem to somehow
Deduce that it must
Be sinful at least to
Simply stop and do
Nothing except to
Just stand there

And even though
We see in our heads
That stepping aside is
Not only a good idea

And even though we
May have preached it
Near many others both
Friend and foe we still
Do not accept or even
Dare one say have the
Courage to admit that
Insight simply is not
Conversion until we
Begin to live by the
Truth that wasting
Time with God is
Really the only
Way to get
Things
Done

Parish Council Meeting: St. Dymphna's Church

Father Realgood: The pastor asked me to sit in for him tonight. As you know, he's in the hospital. Shall we begin with a prayer?

George Grugg (aside to Ima Christian): At least he doesn't have his guitar.

Father Realgood and others: "…and deliver us from evil. Amen."

Sam Stearns: As council president, I officially call to order the 483rd meeting of the council. The first order of business will be the formal approval of the parish budget.

Molly Bergen: Aren't we going to talk about it? WHAT IS THIS, A RUBBER STAMP? I demand to have existential input.

Ima Christian: You idiot! We've had thirty-seven meetings on the budget. Where were you?

Father Realgood: Now, now—

Molly Bergen: Well I had ballet class and I missed a few meetings but…

Ima Christian: Vote, vote.

Sam Stearns: All in favor say, "Aye." Ayes have it. Next on the agenda is the Dymphna statue repair. My wife will make the presentation.

Sally Stearns: Terrific, incredible!

Ima Christian: Say good night, Gracie.

Sally Stearns: Pardon me?

Ima Christian: Nothing, Kid, go ahead.

Sally Stearns: I move that we repair Dymphna's knee—it was broken when Father Realgood, er, I mean, SOMEONE, hit a baseball which hit the statue.

George Grugg: I demand to know if it was done on purpose. Does Father "Slugger" want to respond?

Ima Christian: Oh, George, get off your dead soapbox. It was an accident.

(Motion to repair passed on voice vote.)

Sam Stearns: For the record, I commend the liturgy committee for this past year's work and for their sensitivity to all viewpoints. Any new business?

George Grugg: I think we ought to pass out antacids to everyone when certain priests preach.

Ima Christian: That soapbox is getting taller, George, I move we table it.

Sam Stearns: All in favor...Ayes have it. Anything else? Ima?

Ima Christian: I move we send a get well card to the pastor.

The meeting was adjourned after this last motion passed on an 8 to 7 vote.

The Biggest Smile on Earth
(17th Sunday, Ordinary time)

Sometimes what
Seems too simple or
Too obvious really is
The most significant
Feature of an event like
The one we have named
The multiplication of loaves
And fishes as if it were some
Kind of math contest or magic
For even if we admit the story
Is rich in symbol and sign
Once we recognize this
Memo about presence
And Eucharist still we
Must also see what is
In plain sight

For while there is
Again the use of food
As a marvelous metaphor
Both for the Kingdom and
For the abundance of gifts
Granted by the Master we
May also need to look at
How while most of the
World goes hungry the
Food problem here is
Not starvation but an
Epidemic of
Obesity

And yet maybe the
Most obvious lesson
Could be seen by giving

Some attention to the boy
Who handed over his food
Since you know he must
Have looked in awe as his
Food grew to feed so many
And then it also seems quite
Probable that the Lord would
Likely have insisted that the
Boy then transport the twelve
Baskets of leftovers so that
When he finally got home
His family saw on
His grinning face
The biggest
Smile on
Earth

Thoughts While Awaiting a New Pastor

I wonder if he likes the early Mass?
Will he be as nice to live with as Ray?
I wonder if he is part Irish or all Irish?
Does he believe strongly in religious education?
He looks very distinguished.
Perhaps he doesn't mind the early Mass.
Will he alternate the writing in the bulletin?
I wonder if he knows how great this parish is.
What TV news does he watch?
Will he bring his dog with him?
Does he share responsibility with others?
Maybe he always gets up early.
I understand he's a professionally trained marriage counselor!
Will he believe me when I tell him I've stored up vacation time from
   the past three years? Two years?
Does he like pizza?
Maybe if everybody told him they always wanted him to say the
   early Mass…
Welcome, welcome, welcome.

The Creative Take-out Food
(18th Sunday, Ordinary time)

It is obvious
But still somehow
Amazing that in culture
After culture sharing food
Continues to have so much
Meaning and significance
For whether in good times
Or in bad we share our
Joys and sorrows in
And around food
From a common
And familiar
Table

But in that famous
Outdoor meal where the
Master broke and shared
Bread with many people
He also told them that He
Was the real fare they
Should take for food
And if they did they
Would have life like
None of them could
Even imagine but
The words must
Have seemed
Quite strange
As they first
Heard him
Speak
Them

And how much
Tougher would it
All appear as it began
To sink in that they were
To take both nutrition and
Life from His table so they
Could bring Good News
To many others since
This chef demanded
That they not only be
Guests but servers
Too who would
Deliver to the
Whole world
This creative
Take-out
Food

You

When I think of you
More often now
Than before
My thinking turns
Toward thanking
My God for you

When I pray for you
More often now
Than before
My prayers
Are prayers of joy

When I'm filled with joy
More often now
Than before
My God gifts me with peace
And the gentleness
Of His favor

When my God favors me
More often now
Than before
He changes my world
And my world
Will never be the same
Ever
Because of you

Magnificent Murmuring
(19th Sunday, Ordinary time)

Put in plain words
The subdued form of
The art called whining is
Named murmuring which
Really is nothing more
Than simple grumbling
Mumbled just loud
Enough to get some
Attention but not
Punishment

In plainer words
It is almost always
Those chosen ones
With less reason to be
Unhappy or hungry who
Seem to have refined the
Skill of clearly expressing
Deep pity for self and the
Alleged forlorn state one
Imagines being stuck in
And still this full bodied
Whine can serve a
Purpose beyond
Any belief

For it does get the
Attention of many of
Us as we hear about a
Murmuring about a sign
Expressed by more than a
Few who had just seen the
Loaves and fishes thingie
Since even as we begin to

Reproach them internally
The Master responds with
Words that force them
To admit that they and
Not He are the obstacle
And since they are us
And we too are them
Maybe our first act
Of honest humility
Results from His
Answer to their
Magnificent
Murmuring

Ireland's People

So many stories
Are told
About the people
Of this land

Most of the words
Would never threaten
The perceiving power
Of an injured organization
So superficial
Are they

Some of the tales
Are true
In part at least
The ones about guilt
And thirst
And banshee worlds

Yet beneath
The jokes and
Clown charges
Lives a people
Of faith
Integrity
And a blazing passion
For freedom from
Oppressors and ugliness

For this people
Have married this land
And from the first breath
Of life
They understand
That Ireland

Is not really a country
But
It's a state of mind
And the heart beat
Of one's soul

Wonder Bread
(20th Sunday, Ordinary time)

For hundreds upon
Many hundreds of years
We have argued about the
Sense of his proclamation
That he is the Bread of Life
Since some said it means
His word is wisdom and
The bread is just symbol
While others thought the
Bread is real presence
And many simply said
The Bread of Life is both
Word and sacrament
And this is Jesus

And still today
That same quarrel is
Behind some modern
Voices who accept Him
As their personal savior
But not as redeemer of
All humanity and others
Even let politics direct
Their faith instead of
The other way around
And some base their
Bread belief on law
Instead of love and
Their life eternal
Begins not now
But only in some
Future planet
Beyond the
Clouds

Yet He says this
Gift from heaven
Is here now and is
Not just a sign or a
Symbolic plaything
Conveying wisdom
But instead this is
Him yes really Him
Yes really His flesh
And truly His blood
Making Him really
Yes really the
Only true
Wonder
Bread

First Impressions

Author: There's something I want to tell you.
Reader: So tell it.
Author: But it's just first impressions.
Reader: Big deal, so tell it already!
Author: I'm trying, if you'd just...
Reader: TELL IT!!
Author: OK, OK, relax.
Reader: (lips, don't unpurse)
Author: It seems like a friendly place.
Reader: That's it? That's your big insight?
Author: I knew you wouldn't like it.
Reader: I like it. I like it. But what's the big deal?
Author: Well, friendliness is part of hospitality and hospitality is maybe the most important virtue of a parish.
Reader: I knew you'd sneak in some theology.
Author: Clever, huh?
Reader: Not really, but it's what I've come to expect.
Author: At least I think it's clever.
Reader: Good, I think.
Author: See ya.
Reader: You got it.

Security for Our Last Homeland
(21st Sunday, Ordinary time)

When we and
Others become fearful
We do some crazy things
Like maybe razing a village
So that we might save it or
By eliminating some of the
Freedoms we say we are
Trying to safeguard and so
When Jesus claims to be
The bread of life and says
We can have life that
Will never ever end
Instead of staying
We are tempted
To walk away
And put Him
And His way
Behind us

It is almost as if
Some cloud invades
Our heads and hearts
So we settle on flight
Instead of confidence
Or we claim paralysis
With wounded pride
Rather than honest
Puzzlement about
What exactly He
Might mean

And still
In the end maybe
The disciples and

Peter had the only
Response that makes
Some sense for where
Else on this earth would
We too go if we truly
Wanted security
For our last
Homeland

Prayer for Peace
in the Mideast

Lord
We are at it again
And again
It's not simple
O, there are those
Who think it's only
About oil
And consumer hunger
And it is
In part

But it's also
About justice
And short term
Force to hold off
Long term slaughter
But now
It's so different
Since
August of '45
And '65 and '70

For no longer
Do we think
Any war
Will end all
War
Or violence
Solves any
Thing
Big or not
Big

But, Lord
How do
We choose life
In the midst of chaos
Of Arab, Israeli
East and west

While awaiting wisdom
We pray protect
Our men and women
Serving there
And theirs' too
And everyone's
Children

Amen

My Goat Knows...
(22nd Sunday, Ordinary time)

Replacing responsible
Living with a sameness
Mandated from above can
Lead to order and law and
Boundaries sort of secure
But when leadership trades
Compassion for regulations
It also means hearts will
Be broken apart for then
The Word is undeniably
Covered and hidden
In a cloak of rules
That starves those
Who are not
In power

And it is almost a
Miracle as great even
As the loaves and fishes
That even though we know
This story about those old
Hypocrites who put a great
Burden on many others by
Ordering strict adherence
As the way and the truth
And the life and thus
Making it impossible
To take the road of
Love we still plunge
Into the very same
Ambush and fail
Again to calm
Any besieged
Heart or
Soul

But perhaps a
Beginning would be
For us to finally start over
By confessing that we have
Messed up again every bit
As much as any arrogant
Groupie mishearing the
Song Michael Rows
The Boat Ashore as
My Goat Knows
The Bowling
Score

An Unfinished Prayer After War

God of power and mercy
We give thanks
That the guns
and bombs
Are silent now

We pray in silence
For those who died
Too young
Too innocent
Too vulnerable
Ours
And theirs

For all humans
We ask forgiveness
That solutions
Come from war
Even if it seemed
Not wrong
Forgive us
Our lack of peace

May we promise
Again
And
Again
To try to
Live with justice
And peace
For you
Are
Peace

For thine is
The power
And
The…
And…

Sign Language
(23rd Sunday, Ordinary time)

One of the truly
Great experiences of a
Lifetime might be the chance
To witness a real pro signing
During the liturgy for those
Among us who are deaf or
Have impaired hearing for
It looks like a miracle as
The signer can generally
Anticipate the sound
Emanating from the
Preacher speaker
Or musician

Besides being a great
Wonderful help for those
Who cannot hear well this
Relatively modern addition
To communication is still
Even more important as a
Metaphor for the closed
Ears of every one of us
Since the Lord reminds
Us again and again and
Yet again that we need
Ears that will hear the
Good News given that
Many who did listen as
He first spoke about a
Kingdom of his Father
Still sauntered away
As if not hearing a
Word He said even
The very moment
Before

And maybe all of
His pleas that we have
Ears and hearts that are
Finally open can only be
Fulfilled when we realize
That it is neither gestures
Nor even hand signals but
Kindness and compassion
Which continue to be the
Only sign language that
Will irrevocably unwrap
Our hearts and our
Ears to hear

Never Again?

The news at night
And in the A.M.
Repeats the horror
Of neighbor
Killing former friends

The rest of Europe
Sits back
As they did before
Partly out of confusion
But partly perhaps
Out of indifference

Yes there's no
Easy answer
But surely
Somehow genocide
Should be noticed
Or is Dachau etc.
Forgotten

The Devil in the Mirror
(24th Sunday, Ordinary time)

Peter must have felt
A little betrayed
When after he gave
That great answer
When Jesus asked
What the grapevine
Said about him
And then gave
Good advice
Rejecting death talk
Still the Master
Called him satan

For certainly
Peter and the others
Must have seen
Hints of the victory
Over sickness and evil
And looked forward
To being on the
Winning side in life
For a change
And a break from
Goodness fatigue
After helping
Helping helping
Every time they
Turned around

So when the Master
Insisted that He
Would be executed
Of course
Peter objected

But then like a
Slap in the face
Was informed that
He still needed to get
Back into discipleship
And learn again
That this Master
Was not kidding
About barriers
On the road of
Love

A Few Words About Forgetting

This past week there was a five part series on TV about the Watergate affair many years ago. I mentioned it to a friend who is in her twenties.

She didn't remember it and wrote it off as just another sleazy "political thing." I tried to explain to her that there was a time when presidents were more respected and that all politicians were not considered crooked. She didn't understand, because she was ignorant of her own history. Watergate was perhaps the most serious threat to our constitution since its adoption.

We are still facing the ramifications of Watergate. That president's political party has still not recovered and is now controlled by a fringe element. Interestingly, in some states the opposite party has also been taken over by fringe zealots, as ordinary people of both parties have become uninvolved.

After talking with my friend, I realized again the importance that our Jewish citizens always place on not forgetting the Holocaust and why they resent it when anything else is called a "holocaust." I also realize why in all of our Christian history, one of the most frequently used words in our prayers has always been "remember."

Empty of Every Alibi
(25th Sunday, Ordinary time)

It is uncanny how
Just about anywhere
On this earth when some
Disputes between nations
Move toward conflict often
The talk disguises the pain
To come by using little and
Almost soothing words
As if that might make
Combat sound more
Like some athletic
Or cooking
Contest

But the Master
Will have none of that
Variety of deception so
Even after the disciples
Had the normal dreaming
About power they would
Have after a huge victory
Over all opposing forces
This Leader speaks not
With soothing words
Regarding some sort
Of victory but speaks
Instead about defeat
And even a death
That most would
Find quite
Shameful

And if that were not
Enough bad news He

Then suggested that
They will only be able
To understand if they
Become like the little
Children among them
Not just because they
Were filled with awe
But because indeed
They were the most
Vulnerable with
Hearts open
For Him and
Empty of
Every
Alibi

Who or What Should We Be Willing to Die For?

One of the most used phrases during the pre-invasion rhubarb last week was that "Haiti is not worth one drop of American blood!" It makes you wonder if it's worth German blood, French blood, Australian blood, or does it have to be blood from a non-Caucasian?

We have come pretty far from fighting and dying for freedom twice this century in Europe, twice in Asia, and so on. Some, perhaps most, would argue that Haiti is not about freedom, or that we can never trust our government again, since Watergate and Vietnam.

Still, it does make me wonder what we Americans are willing to risk death for. If Haiti were Ireland or Germany or England, would those opponents be more willing to fight? Is it because Haitians are dark-skinned that we are reluctant to invade?

It seems clear that we want to know that our national interest is at stake. Do we not also need to clarify if we are slipping into a new isolationism? Obviously the issues are complicated. But if the most powerful nation only worries about itself, to whom do weaker people turn for help?

A Christian Hokey Pokey
(26th Sunday, Ordinary time)

Hey there you
Super scripture storyteller
Listen up here and explain
This gospel so that it is clear
To those of us not in your
Inner circle for this
Master seems a bit
Unhinged in this
Strange tale

For first He
Demands that we
Allow some who are not
Really part of us to do stuff
That we thought only we
Had the power and grace
To do and accomplish and
Then He rants on us for
Some of the problems
We still have
Being human
And all that
You know

It seems like
We need to be
Inclusive in our
Acceptance of others
Who are on the outside
Looking in but at the same
Time He demands that we be
Ferocious with ourselves for
Some of the problems
We still have

Being human
And all that
You know

So does it have
To be that way that
We be tougher on ourselves
Than on any others at the very
Same time because it seems
So unfair to do some of
This and some of that
So it does appear
That He wants us
To dance to some
Kind of Christian
Hokey Pokey

Really, Really, Really Obscene Words

Why can't you be like your brother?
I wish you hadn't been born.
Drop dead.
She is our slow one.
Marry wealthy.
I wish you were a girl.
You dummy.
Anger is not allowed.
Shut up! I deserve one more drink.
It's always your fault.
Keep on like that and you'll end up like your uncle.
You drive me to drink.
You're so slow.
We are not put on earth to have fun.

These phrases or comments are all too often routine within our homes. They are way more obscene than #%*&^@%^#$@*&(!

A Jesus Makeover
(27th Sunday, Ordinary time)

The fact that
We seem destined
To always be trying to
Reconstruct God over and
Over again in our very own
Image or likeness and even
Often basing the theology
On an English translation
Of a Greek text truly is
Amusing but only in a
Pitifully pathetic way
For our own arrogant
Certainty in matters
Such as these will
Always end up with
People being hurt

And even though
Hurting others does not
Seem to be central even
To a Messiah who speaks
English we still seem to be
Able to get it wrong as we
Look at sayings said to be
From Jesus himself about
Divorce or even marriage
For like an actor knowing just
One step of one dance we
Often choose to berate and
Belittle any model that does
Not fit into our redesigned
Messiah or Holy Sender

Perhaps we just
Need to remember that
It was the riff raff of the earth
Who understood Him best and
Did listen to His word enough
To understand that there was
Always room at His table for
Any who sinned or had love
And not law at the center of
The heart of faith for
They never had any
Even tiny need
For a Jesus
Makeover

The Ghosts of the Robber Barons

The eighteenth
And the nineteenth centuries
Were the playland
For these original
Baron capitalists
As millions upon millions
Fell to them
And little to those who
Labored for them

Some new understandings
And the club
Of bargaining together
Curbed the excesses
For most of this last half century
Until now of all times

It is respectable
Again
To blame the poor
Or those without homes
Even those coming
From foreign lands
Are seen as the problem
And the ghosts of the barons
Have begun to smile
Again

Get Outta Town
(28th Sunday, Ordinary time)

The story about
The man who came
To Jesus asking what
He should do to inherit
The elusive eternal life
Evolves so neatly that
It is almost as if it had
Maybe been written by
Some pundit who likes
Cliffhanger finishes or
At least some sort of
Surprise at the end
Even if it is not a
Happy one

But at least the
Man in the story was
Disappointed and sad
But not really surprised
That some demands were
Made by this preacher for
He knew that to live a life
That would be spiritual or
At least religious would
Mean some surrender
But the area asked for
Was way beyond his
Wants or desire

Yet the same
Demand given us
Would be received
With disbelief and just
A smidgen of ridicule for

We would be so incredibly
Surprised at any notion of
Sacrifice that our reaction
Might not just have been
Negative but instead like
Some worn out stand up
Comedian we might try
To disguise our panic
By assuming he was
Kidding so then we
Could snicker or
Just shout and
Say a big hey
Funny man
Get outta
Town

Maybe

She was armed
Or so it seemed
As she appeared
To hug herself
While waiting for
The ONE WHO
HAD TO HEAR HER

How could you make
Jokes at the end
Like you just did
And not for the first time
Have you no sense
Of decorum or at least
Concern for we who
Come here to adore

Knowing that a quip
Even one well constructed
Would only fuel
The flames of her
Righteous faith
That never leaves room
Even for a tiny
Teensy smile
The ONE WHO
HAD TO HEAR
Simply
Humbly
Or so he thought
Simply said
Maybe

A Guaranteed Promotion
(29th Sunday, Ordinary time)

There seem to be
Two types of people
Who end up being in
Leadership positions
In our various human
Institutions and groups
And the most obvious are
Those ambitious ones who
Also are able to easily walk
Over others on their way up
Since they appear to be
Short at least a brick
Or two in the ethics
Department

But just as
Easily advanced
May be the ones who
Appear lacking in ambition
But use a kind of imitation
Humility to disguise poor
Self esteem and the fear
That success will never
Happen in their chosen
Field and while often
Not noisy they still
Might quietly
Climb higher
And higher

The problem is that
Neither raging ambition
Nor phony meekness are
On-the-job descriptions for

Any leaders demanded
By Jesus of Nazareth
And instead it seems
Quite clear that serving
Others is not just the
Way to greatness in
The Kingdom of God
It is certainly the
Only way to a
Guaranteed
Promotion

Connemara

If there is an end
To the world
Or at least an edge
It must be very much
Like Connaugt

Its land is rock
And its hills
Epitomize emptiness
Or bleakness
At least

Yeats had it right
In "terrible beauty"
As did thousands
Who knew its majesty
But who needed nurture
And food
So left finally
This gorgeous hell

The Bartimaeus Problem
(30th Sunday, Ordinary time)

The old saying
That we should be
Careful about what we
Seek or pray for seems
Particularly true when the
One we ask is stronger and
Bigger than King Kong or
Any other characters we
Use to keep ourselves
Amused and even a
Little bit frightened
So we do not even
Have to come
Near them

And when it
Comes to faith rather
Than movies we seem to
Know it might be easier to
Not have our eyes or hearts
Opened for then we would
See the world as it is and
Could no longer pretend
That we were not just
Staying blind on
Purpose

And Mark makes it
Clear that once we did
Understand that the man
Could ask for anything and
Since his daring wish to see
Was quickly granted that also
Means this would be true too

For anyone who asks for this
Same gift of sight and then
Forever after we would not
Be able to be delusional
And reproach God if we
Are afraid to ask to see
Since we can never
Explain away the
Bartimaeus
Problem

Glendalough

The wind was wild
That day
I first came
To see where Kevin
Set down

The tower
So old and so filled
With the majesty of ages
The church
Where Kevin said his Abba
Both seize the visitor
And like the wind
Bring bumpiness
To the skin

Yet it is the land
And hills
And water
That give peace

The Inner Puppy
(31st Sunday, Ordinary time)

Even at our worst
When we almost believe
The world is jinxed
Or at least turned
Slightly against us and
Evil too threatens
Now and then
Another reality
Hints at still
Something else

For inside us also
Is the response
We share with
The scribe
Who was not far
From the kingdom
Since our
Inner puppy
To use a more
Or less
Precise term
Is full of the
Heroic energy
Of loving with the
Whole heart
And mind
And body

And if
All we need
To better match
Our internal
Knowledge

With our external
Action
Is a bit more
Schooling in the
Great commandment
Possibly

Our inner puppy
Just needs a
Little more
Obedience
Training

On Hearing of a Heart Attack

The shock
Or surprise
Or whatever this
This dismembered feeling is
Even nudges out
My usual
Why

He's so young
Does everything
I mean
Everything right
And yet he too
Was tapped from behind
By that shadow
Of death

He's better now
The medical ministers
Mouth
To family
And friends
They are cautious
So cautious but
Not without hope

His friends too
Will begin
Giving birth
To hope
Probably soon
But never
Ever will forget
The moment
They heard
The news

The Width of a Single Hair
(32nd Sunday, Ordinary time)

Most of us
Just hate it when
Someone gives us
A piece of news
That might make us
Change something
About how we live
So often we presume
That the news was meant
For someone else

And quite like the
Rich one giving only
From his surplus
We can put distance
Between the poor widow
And our non-poor selves
And applaud her gift
As we jeer the scribes
And the stingy rich

Yet sometime
This side of heaven
We may realize that
We can no longer
Pretend that grace
Is measured in money
Or even success
For we are both the
Widow and the scribe

And just as it is not
Up to us to decide
Which of the poor

Are deserving of
Our bequest
So too it is not our call
To not be a giver
However impoverished
We think we are
For the distance between
Humility and pride
Is the width of
A single
Hair

Still Another Golfer's Prayer

Lord, I know it's no disgrace to shoot 120,
but it's no great privilege either.
In the vastness of your universe and the
attention given to plague, pestilence and war
is there not room somewhere for my plea for
a lower score?
Is it not possible just once to give me
a round without slice or hook or the
snickers of my partners, WHO ALMOST
ALWAYS PLAY BETTER THAN I?
Even if my request is slightly out of line,
not least because you've heard it again and again,
could you at least try to influence the USGA
so that pastors can always take a mulligan?

Thank you, Amen.

Scary Stuff
(33rd Sunday, Ordinary time)

Now and again
When we have to listen
One more time to those odd
Tales complete with images
About the end times surely
Our temptation often must
Be to run away just as fast
As our handsome legs can
Carry us since we still
Mistakenly read it as
An incredibly bad
Description or
Prediction

But the most
Useful strategy might
Be refusing to reduce the
Gospel to only one period
From long ago and far away
And as one alternative let it
Speak with every generation
Including even our own for
The delight is in discovering
Again that these writings and
This part of Mark were meant
To be comfort food to soothe
And console like ice cream
Or the favorite cookies
Of our sensible God
Chocolate chip
Of course

And the lesson
Mark gives through

The fig tree could not
Be more gentle or more
Filled with the promise of
Celebration and festivity
As it brings hope today
Since the victory and
Reality of the Son
Never would or
Could ever be
Any kind of
Scary
Stuff

Presider Greeting Images

That family in the front
Seems happy today
Thank God
For the last year
Has been hell piled on hell
For them
With death and despair
And joblessness
Journeying almost daily
Into their home
Maybe, just maybe
The darkness is fading

On the other side
Down a few rows
Is the man who looks
Like a judge
Who's always pleasant
As he weighs
The biblical truths
He loves so much

The young woman next to him
Seems more serene
Than she has
Since her engagement
Was broken
Bitterly for her
Though perhaps
Better for her too

That couple
Half-way down next to the
Contemplative octogenarian
On the other side

Still haven't smiled
Since I've known them
And always look
Like they'd be more
Comfortable with a god
Who's angry
Or vengeful
Or at least a little
Thirsty for blood

The children
Across the aisle
Are filled with wonder
And boredom
With delight
And devilishness today
Reminding us of
The joy/pain of youth

How many words
Will these faithful
Hear today
Or can the messenger
Even find a way
Since he cannot sing
Play guitar
Or even dance
Very well
And well it is
That it all depends on Him
Instead
Of
Us

Jesus the Turtle
(Feast of Christ the King)

Although it
Probably does not
Make much difference
In the end the title king
Does not find very many
Friendly minds or hearts
Today since they are no
Longer part of the lives
Of very many people
Almost anywhere
Anymore

So though we might
Prefer to keep our gods
Out of sight and mind still
We do not choose to see
Our divine mentor as an
Irrelevant monarch nor
For sure do we want to
Let Him get very close
To us where we might
Have to have at least
An equal relationship
So we find a way to
Fool ourselves that
Of course we know
He is not snobbish
For He says He is
Very close to us
But we do try
To keep Him
Without any
Influence

So we mostly
Domesticate Him like
A low maintenance pet
For we still do not allow
Ourselves to appreciate
That He really is the one
Who will always love us
And still give Himself
For us even though
We do sell Him and
Ourselves short as
We resist Him as
Brother and keep
Him tame as
Jesus the
Turtle

The Gospel According to Simeon
(Presentation of the Lord)

Sometimes
We get so caught up
In the drama of a gospel
That we can forget that an
Event like the presentation
Is not an eyewitness account
But simply and profoundly
A nice attempt to teach the
Point of view of this author
Who reminds us that the
Anointed one arrived and
Was presented as other
Needy children were
Because He came to
Preach good news
To the poor

The simple
Offering of pigeons
Stood out in contrast
To the donations of the
Better set of believers
And yet in the end the
Ultimate gift surely was
One given to the child
In the word of Simeon
And way more valuable
Than any gold or wealth
As he set the stage for
This child to grow and
Become the source of
Joy and pain beyond
Words or description

For most people
Everywhere

And even though
The words about this
Unique child of God
Would be understood
Later and only in part
It was still clear that
This one was special
So at the time one
Can only wonder
If the old man
Knew he had
Just begun
The gospel
According
To Simeon

The Only One He Had Ever Knowed
(Feast of the Dedication of the Lateran Basilica in Rome)

Sometimes one can
Be fooled and go down a
Road too frequently traveled
Like for instance when we look at
A beautiful structure so brilliantly
Built for worship that we might
Conclude that this community
Also is therefore beautiful
And gifted or even
Virtuous as well
As good

But when both
Eyes are opened and
Then reality sinks in that
Even though they are terribly
And incredibly important still
Neither a temple nor even a
Fresh and new church building
Can be the central focus since
The real treasure will always
Be the cathedral of the heart
And the basilica of the Spirit
As we too continue to
Bask in the love of
The Father and
Of the Son

So when the Master
Goes after the hypocrites
Selling and soiling various
Places and corners where
They worship He also was
Confronting us for not seeing

Our own flaws in them too and
So that surely is as dense as a
Pastor who was so proud and
Delighted when the little boy
Told him that he was the
Very bestest priest he had
Ever knowed that it took
This prophet a while to
Understand that the
Important truth was
That he was also
The only one
The little boy
Had ever
Knowed

Walking among the Graves
(Feast of the Ascension)

One of the more
Instructive experiences
Anyone on earth can have
Turns out to be a stroll in a
Significantly old cemetery
Especially if the writing
Resting on the stones is
Still able to be read
And if a loved one is
Buried there

For depending on
The mood when viewing
The inscriptions and dates
Etched into the stone one is
Furious about a life ended
Too soon or alternatively
Delighted with the ones
Who made it through a
Century as story after
Story after story runs
Through the mind
When the walker
Knows those
Buried there

From shaking
Our fists at the God
Who allowed loved ones
To leave us for some world
As yet not seen and wanting
To screech when a heaven is
Referred to even for a second
To the joyous remembering of

The laughter and gifted heart
Of those who speak now but
Only by way of reminiscence
We do seem to bounce from
Grief to joy yet end up like
A little child afraid of the
Dark because he knows
With certainty that
Someone is there

And yet we sense that
The time is not wasted
For we realize that we
Will go where He has
And one day will see
Those coming later
Cursing or laughing
As they are walking
Among the graves

Looking for a Double Cross
(Feast of the Exaltation of the Holy Cross)

Why questions
Are usually the ones
Which get us into trouble
With some shaky leaders or
Perhaps even into a mess of
Distress within ourselves if
We are one of the chosen
Ones who use internal
Word games to avoid
Coming to terms with
Our own demons
Or personal
Anxieties

And maybe that
Really is why even
Today the cross is
So difficult for us to
Understand or accept
So we focus more on
Wondering why and how
Any father could knowingly
Pressure his son to undergo
Such an unsacred and awful
Death before mostly people
Who did not even know him
And as we play this game
Once again we still refuse
To just look at the open
Arms on the cross and
Simply accept that
He did it for us
For His love is
That immense

And not too
Good to
Be true

And even today
We still will not
Always even see
The great love on
That awful hill for
Our internal game
Always seems to
Force us to keep
On looking for
A double
Cross

The Kiss of Life
(All Souls' Day)

When death is no
Longer an abstraction
Because it finally hits home
So cruelly that we can barely
Put one foot in front of the other
Or even remember to breathe
Then all of the familiar and
Shallow sayings about
Passing over or being
In a better place now
Not only lose logic
They also usually
Incite anger

But even after
We are able to move
Beyond the desperate
Silence that relocates into
Our hearts as we try to adjust
To the voiceless presence of
Our loved ones still the words
And the slogans around death
Continue to haunt and taunt
For a very long time unless
And until a different faith
Replaces our shattered
Hopes centered on and
Around the belief that
Seems to have
So deeply let
Us down

And yet perhaps
As we begin to laugh

Again even at jokes that
Arrive dead as a doornail
It might be the first hint
That we are beginning to
See that the pledge of a
Life without end was not
Simply a campaign ploy
But a real promise that
One day we will know
Without doubt that
The kiss of death
Has become now
And forever
The kiss
Of life

Order Form

Please copy this page, add the necessary information, and mail it with your check or money order, payable to *Musings*, to:

> Musings
> PO Box 343
> Cedar, MN 55011

ISBN: 1-930374-20-8
Musings from Michael $20.00 each   Qty. _____

Total: _____

MN residents add 6.5% sales tax ($1.30/book) _____

Shipping: $3.00 first book, $1.50 each additional _____

Total enclosed: _____

Name: _____

Address: _____

City: _____ State: _____ Zip: _____

Phone: (__) _____ Email:_____

You can also order this book securely from DeForest Press at www.DeForestPress.com, or by calling toll-free 1-877-441-9733.